UTOPIA

UTOPIA

THOMAS MORE

Introduction by China Miéville
Essays by Ursula K. Le Guin

VERSO
London • New York

First published by Verso 2016
© Verso 2016
The text of More's *Utopia* (1516) is based on the Cassell &
Company edition of 1901, edited by David Price
Introduction © China Miéville 2016
Essays © Ursula K. Le Guin

'The Limits of Utopia' was originally published in
Salvage #1: Amid This Stony Rubbish, 2015.
'A Non-Euclidean View of California as a Cold Place to Be' was originally
published in *Dancing at the Edge of the World* (New York: Grove Press, 1989).
'A War Without End' and 'The Operating Instructions' were originally
published in *The Wave in the Mind* (Boston: Shambhala, 2004).

1 3 5 7 9 10 8 6 4 2

Verso
UK: 6 Meard Street, London W1F 0EG
US: 20 Jay Street, Suite 1010, Brooklyn, NY 11201
versobooks.com

Verso is the imprint of New Left Books

ISBN-13: 978-1-78478-760-8
ISBN-13: 978-1-78478-761-5 (US EBK)
ISBN-13: 978-1-78478-759-2 (UK EBK)

British Library Cataloguing in Publication Data
A catalogue record for this book is available from the British Library

Library of Congress Cataloging-in-Publication Data
A catalog record for this book is available from the Library of Congress

Typeset in Fournier MT by Hewer Text UK Ltd, Edinburgh
Printed in the UK by CPI Group (UK) Ltd, Croydon, CR0 4YY

Contents

PART I:
INTRODUCTION

by China Miéville

1
Close to the Shore

—⟫◆⟪—

If you know from where to set sail, with a friendly pilot offering expertise, it should not take you too long to reach Utopia.

Since the first woman or man first yearned for a better place, dreamers have dreamed them at the tops of mountains and cradled in hidden valleys, above clouds and deep under the earth – but above all they have imagined them on islands. The island utopia has been a standard since antique times: Eusebius's Panchaea and Iambulus's Islands of the Sun; Henry Neville's Isle of Pines, and Antangil, from the 1616 novel of that name; Bacon's Bensalem; Robert Paltock's Nosmnbdsgrutt, from *Peter Wilkins*; Huxley's Pala; Austin Tappan Wright's Islandia; and countless more. And in the centre of that great archipelago of dissent and hope, one place, one name, looms largest.

This island, this book, is the paradigm. 'More's *Utopia*', in the words of the scholar Roland Greene, 'is perhaps the text that establishes insularity as an early modern vantage [and] introduces a way of thinking that is properly called utopian', defined by 'a multifarious phenomenon which I will call island logic'.

But, to repeat, it is not a long voyage to get there. Citizens of More's Utopia 'keep up the art of navigation', pass back and forth on various tasks, trading surpluses of 'corn, honey, wool, flax, wood, wax, tallow, leather, and cattle . . . to other nations'. Only the thinnest stretch of ocean separates Utopia from the mainland. For somewhere so famously and constitutively *nowhere*, this no-place Utopia is very close to the shore.

And there's a more startling surprise with regard to its island-ness, a fact of which not nearly enough is generally made:

> [T]his was no island at first, but a part of the continent. Utopus, that conquered it . . . brought the rude and uncivilised inhabitants into . . . good government . . . Having soon subdued them, he designed to separate them from the continent, and to bring the sea quite round them. To accomplish this he ordered a deep channel to be dug . . . and that the natives might not think he treated them like slaves, he not only forced the inhabitants, but also his own soldiers, to labour in carrying it on. As he set a vast number of men to work, he, beyond all men's expectations, brought it to a speedy conclusion. And his neighbours, who at first laughed at the folly of the undertaking, no sooner saw it brought to perfection than they were struck with admiration and terror.

This most famous example of the island utopia, the ideal-type itself, is not by nature an island at all. The fifteen miles of water that keep it apart from the main body politic are not there by God's will, but by the sweat of native people, among others, digging at an invading conqueror's command. The splendid – utopian – isolation is part of the violent imperial spoils.

The classic reactionary attack on the utopian impulse is that it is, precisely, no place, impossibly distant. But, disavowed and right there, in More's foundation myth of the dream polity is a very different unease: that, wrought by brutality, coerced from above, it is all too close.

There could be no one better suited to frame More's foundational text than that great dissident utopian and dissident-utopian thinker, Ursula K. Le Guin. In her words from 'Utopiyin, Utopiyang', which follows More's text in this book, 'Every utopia since *Utopia*' – at least – 'has also been, clearly or obscurely, actually or possibly, in the author's or in the readers' judgement, both a good place and a bad one. Every eutopia contains a dystopia, every dystopia contains a eutopia.'

These contradictions thrive in single heads as easily as between them, and in the texts those heads produce. The interminable debates about what More 'really' meant miss this obvious fact, and are thus of as much use as any other discussion of 'actual' artistic or political 'intent' that treats it as a given or a secret to be decoded. Which is to say: some, but not much.

Was More's utopia blueprint, or satire, or something else? As if these are exclusive. As if all utopias are not always all of the above, in degrees that vary as much in the context of their reception as of their creation.

The dangerous drive, the dystopia-in-utopia, then, is not only in the impulse, though it can certainly reside there, but in the actuality: that proximity of the island to the shore. Tragedians making their peace with power, liberals loudly warn against utopia*nism* from below (often full of sentimentalism for their own dead radicalism, and lachry-mose at their new realism); alongside them the hard-right radicals of power and oppression dream their own dreams of the good life: supremacist arcadias. And those who rule, more powerful and traditionally less voluble than their apologists, calmly configure and effect utopias of their own. In which those they rule have no choice but to live and serve and die.

These are a few of the limits of utopia (explored in the companion essay of that name that follows this one).

But the fact that the utopian impulse is always stained doesn't mean it can or should be denied or battened down. It is as inevitable as hate and anger and joy, and as necessary. Utopianism isn't hope, still less optimism: it is need, and it is desire. For recognition, like all desire, and/but for the specifics of its reveries and programmes, too; and above all for betterness *tout court*. For alterity, something other than the exhausting social lie. For rest. And when the cracks in history open wide enough, the impulse may even jimmy them a little wider.

We can't do without this book. We are all and have always been Thomas More's children. Even his literary ancestors were also his preemptive descendants, throwing him up, making him a hinge point, so his ditch-demanding king could give their earlier yearnings a name. That we must keep returning to the text, with whatever suspicion, is to honour it. It gave us a formulation, a concept, we needed.

Though it is perhaps past time to rethink that word.

We don't know much of the society that Utopus and his armies destroyed – that's the nature of such forced forgetting – but we know its name. It's mentioned *en* swaggering colonial *passant*, a *hapax legomenon* pilfered from Gnosticism: 'for Abraxa was its first name'. We know the history of such encounters, too; that every brutalised, genocided and enslaved people in history have, like the Abraxans, been 'rude and uncivilised' in the tracts of their invaders.

A start for any habitable utopia must be to overturn the ideological bullshit of empire, and, unsentimentally but respectfully, to revisit the traduced and defamed cultures on the bones of which some conqueror's utopian dreams were piled up. 'Utopia' is to the political imaginary of betterness as 'Rhodesia' is to Zimbabwe, 'Gold Coast' to Ghana. How, then, might we set out for New Abraxa?

'I don't think we're ever going to get to utopia again by going forward', says Le Guin, in 'A Non-Euclidian View of California as a Cold Place to Be'. And so she suggests instead the formula people of the Swampy Cree First Nation have traditionally used in orientation to the future: *Usà puyew usu wapiw!*

'I go backward, look forward', it means. It describes the porcupine, *Erethizon dorsatum*, backing into a rock crevice, from where it can watch for danger ahead. 'In order to speculate safely on an inhabitable future', she says, 'perhaps we would do well to find a rock crevice and go backward.' Far from hyperbolic, the adjective 'inhabitable' seems admirably restrained in the face of the social and ecological degradation of accelerating neoliberalism.

From those rocks, the porcupine can plot its own utopias. And, at least as important, going backward, looking forward, it can try to escape the onrushing utopias of those in power.

But such utopias of the powerful have levelled many landscapes. They're distinguished by their flattening power, by the fields of rubble they leave. What if they sweep up all the rocks and leave none between which to hide? That defensive porcupine gait recalls another. The motion has a counterpart, a poignant inversion, the buffeting of a figure long-since a cliché of radical pessimism, but the endless citation of which (including in 'The Limits of Utopia', here) still can't quite strip it of its power and importance.

Walter Benjamin's angel of history.

His eyes are staring, his mouth is open, his wings are spread . . . His face is turned to the past. Where we perceive a chain of events, he sees one single catastrophe which keeps piling wreckage upon wreckage and hurls it in front of his feet . . . [A] storm . . . blowing from Paradise . . . irresistibly propels him into the future to which his back is turned, while the pile of debris before him grows skyward. This storm is what we call progress.

The porcupine goes backward, looks forward, to see futures – to avoid some, to plan another. The angel goes forward, looks backward, in anguish – plunging towards a future it can't see, mourning pasts it can't redeem.

Which way are the predatory utopias twisting us? Is the porcupine pulled from its broken crevice and wrenched around to hurtle future-ward in their slipstream? Or does the angel manage to catch the walls of the canyon with the tips of its outstretched wings and hold on and turn and wriggle into a place to hide and grit its teeth and face the telos of the wind?

Will the porcupine become the angel, or the angel the porcupine?

Yet again, there's no either/or. The history of all hitherto existing societies – it's been pointed out many times – is a history of monsters, on all sides. Our utopianism is always-already a chimera. *Angelus erethizon*: a porcupine with celestial wings; a seraph bristling with spines.

And like those other hybrids which ultimately overthrew the ghastly utopia that created and despised them, our cousins, the beast-men of More(au), it must learn to move with an unprecedented crossbred gait. To use its parts and powers in ungainly but effective ways. Stilt-walking on wingtips, gripping with the quills of feathers and the quills of a sharper weapon kind. Fighting on four legs, two, and none, and swimming – it's close to the shore – to New Abraxa.

It will move, perhaps, as it is just possible we might, with a new motion neither and both animal and divine.

2

The Limits of Utopia

Dystopias infect official reports.

The Intergovernmental Panel on Climate Change (IPCC) demands a shift in our emissions by a third to avoid utter disaster. KPMG, in the leaden chattiness of corporate powerpoint-ese, sees the same horizon. NASA part-funds a report warning that systemic civilizational collapse 'is difficult to avoid'.

We may quibble with the models, but not that the end of everything is right out there, for everyone to discuss.

The stench and blare of poisoned cities, lugubrious underground bunkers, ash landscapes . . . Worseness is the bad conscience of betterness, dystopias are rebukes integral to the utopian tradition. We hanker and warn, our best dreams and our worst standing together against our waking.

Fuck this up, and it's a desiccated, flooded, cold, hot, dead Earth. Get it right? There are lifetimes'-worth of pre-dreams of New Edens, from le Guin and Piercy and innumerable others, going right back, visions of what, nearly two millennia ago, the Church Father Lactantius, in *The Divine Institutes*, called the 'Renewed World'.

[T]he earth will open its fruitfulness, and bring forth the most abundant fruits of its own accord; the rocky mountains shall drop with honey; streams of wine shall run down, and rivers flow with milk; in short, the world itself shall rejoice, and all nature exult, being rescued and set free from the dominion of evil and impiety, and guilt and error.

And it's never only the world that's in question: for Lactantius, as for all the best utopias, it's humanity too. The world will rejoice because we at last will be capable of inhabiting it, free from the evil and impiety and guilt and error with which we've excoriated it. The relationship between humanity and what we'd now call the environment will be healed.

But so rich a lineage has hardly stopped countless environmentalisms from failing, not merely to change the world, but to change the agenda about changing the world.

We who want another, better Earth are understandably proud to keep alternatives alive in this, an epoch that punishes thoughts of change. We need utopias. That's almost a given in activism. If an alternative to this world were inconceivable, how could we change it?

But utopia has its limits: utopia can be toxic. What price hopelessness, indeed? But what price hope?

In 1985 the city government announced that it would locate a trash incinerator in South Central Los Angeles, a year after California Waste Management paid half a million taxpayers' dollars to the consultancy firm Cerrell Associates for advice on locating such controversial toxic facilities. The Cerrell Report is a how-to, a checklist outlining the qualities of the ' "least resistant" personality profile'. Target the less educated, it advises. The elderly. 'Middle- and higher-soci-oeconomic strata neighborhoods', it says, 'should not fall at least within the one-mile and five-mile radii of the proposed site.'

Target the poor.

That this is the strategy is unsurprising: that they admit it raises eyebrows. 'You know', one wants to whisper, 'that we can hear you?'

In fact the local community did resist, and successfully. But what are sometimes called the Big Ten green groups – the Sierra Club, Friends of the Earth, the National Resources Defense Council, the Wilderness Society, and others – refused the request to join the campaign. Because, they said, it was not an environmental, but a 'community health' issue.

The fallacies of Big Green. Start with heuristics like *rural* versus *urban*, *nature* versus *the social*, and in the face of oppressive power you easily become complicit, or worse, in environmental injustice, in racism. Such simplistic urbopho-bic utopianism can unite the most nostalgic conservative, seeking solace in a national park, with the most extropian post-hippy touting an eco-start-up.

For Lactantius, it was God who would heal a broken nature. This is a more secular age – sort of. But not every-one leaves such messianism aside: some incorporate it into a new, and newly vacuous, totality.

In 1968, Stewart Brand opened the first *Whole Earth Catalogue* with an image of the Blue Planet, Spaceship Earth, a survival pod in which we mutually cuddle. Beside it the text read, 'We are as gods and might as well get good at it.'

Here, says the image, is a beautiful Gaian totality. Here, say the words, is the ecological subject: 'We'. Which obviously leaves unanswered, in the famous punchline to the blistering, uneasy joke, Tonto's question to the Lone Ranger: 'Who is "we"?'

Faced with the scale of what's coming, there's a common and baleful propriety, a self-shackling green politeness. 'Anything', the argument goes, 'is better than nothing.' Hence solutions to tempt business, and the pleading for ecologically inflected economic rationality. Capitalism, we are told by Jonathan Porritt, an eminent British environmentalist, is the only game in town.

And businesses do adapt, according to their priorities. Whatever the barking of their pet deniers, the oil companies all have Climate Change Divisions – less to fight that change than to plan for profit during it. Companies extend into newly monetised territories. Thus the brief biofuels boom, and that supposed solution to the planet's problems drives rapid deforestation and food riots, before the industry and market tank. The invisible hand is supposed to clean up its own mess, with Emissions Trading Schemes and offsetting. Opportunities and incentives for shady deals and inflated baseline estimates increase, as, relentlessly, do the emissions. EU carbon bonds remain junk. New financial instruments proliferate: weather derivatives that make climate chaos itself profitable. What are called 'catastrophe bonds' change hands in vast quantities, because one of the minor casualties of capitalism is shame.

Citizens fret about their own refuse, which we should, absolutely, minimise. But in the UK only 10 per cent of waste is down to households. Recall that the very concept of litter was an invention of the American packaging industry, in 1953, in response to a local ban on disposable bottles. The caul of atomised and privatised guilt under which we're encouraged to labour is a quite deliberate act of misdirection.

At a grander scale, the most conciliatory green organizations obfuscate the nexus of ecological degradation, capitalism and imperialism in which they're caught up. In 2013 the US Environmental Protection Agency presented its National Climate Leadership Award, for 'tackling the challenge of climate change with practical, common-sense, and cost-saving solutions', to Raytheon.

It isn't clear whether Raytheon's drones will be embossed with the award's symbol, so their commitment to sustainability can flash like a proud goldfish fin as they rain death on Afghan villages.

In the service of profit, even husbanding trees supposedly to counteract emissions can be violence. Far worse than merely a failure, UN-backed emission-reduction forest offsetting schemes – known as REDD (Reducing Emissions from Deforestation and Forest Degradation) – legitimate monocultures and seize land, in the name of the planet, all so corporations can continue to pollute. In Uganda, 22,000 farmers are evicted for the UN-accredited New Forests. Company plans. In Kenya, Ogiek people are threatened with violent expulsion from the Mau Forest, in a project blessed by the UN. And in case we need an unsubtle metaphor, the Guaraquecaba Climate Action Project in Brazil, bankrolled by Chevron, General Motors and American Electric Power, locks the Guarani people away from their own forest, and to do so it employs armed guards called 'Força Verde' – *Green Force*.

This is environmentalism as dispossession, what the Indigenous Environmental Network calls Carbon Colonialism.

And stocks of heavy industry go up. The recent IPCC report left financial markets unmoved: the value such markets continue to grant oil, coal and gas reserves ignores the international targets according to which the bulk of such reserves not only are still in the earth, but must remain so. This carbon bubble declaims that the choice is climate catastrophe or another financial one.

Or, of course, both.

Forget any spurious *human* totality: there is a very real, dangerous, other modern totality in commanding place, one with which too much environmentalism has failed to wrestle. As Jason Moore puts it, 'Wall Street is a way of organizing Nature.'

The very term 'Anthropocene', which gives with one hand, insisting on human drivers of ecological shift, misleads with its implied 'We'. After all, whether in the deforestation of what's now Britain, the extinction of the megafauna in North America, or any of countless other examples, *Homo sapiens*, *anthropos*, has always fed back into its -*cene*, the ecology of which it is constituent, changing the world. Nor was what altered to make these previously relatively local effects planetary and epochal, warranting a new geochronological term, the birth (as if, in too many accounts, by some miracle) of heavy industry, but a shift in the political economy by which it and we are organised, an accelerating cycle of profit and accumulation.

Which is why Moore, among others, insists that this epoch of potential catastrophe is not the 'Anthropocene', but the 'Capitalocene'.

Utopias are necessary. But not only are they insufficient: they can, in some iterations, be part of the ideology of the system, the bad totality that organises us, warms the skies, and condemns millions to peonage on garbage scree.

The utopia of togetherness is a lie. Environmental justice means acknowledging that there is no whole earth, no 'we', without a 'them'. That we are not all in this together.

Which means fighting the fact that fines for toxic spills in predominantly white areas are five times what they are in minority ones. It means not only providing livings for people who survive by sifting through rejectamenta in toxic dumps but squaring up against the imperialism of garbage that put them there, against trash neoliberalism by which poor countries compete to become repositories of filth.

And it means standing directly against military power and violence. Three times as many land-rights and environmental activists were murdered in 2012 as a decade before. Environmental justice means facing down Shell not only for turning Nigeria's Ogoniland into a hallucinatory sump, a landscape of petrochemical Ragnarök, but for arming the Nigerian state for years, during and after the rule of Sani Abacha.

Arms trading, dictatorships and murder are environmental politics.

Those punching down rely not on the quiescence, but on the *weakness* of those against whom they fight. The Cerrell Report is clear: 'All socioeconomic groupings tend to resent the nearby siting of major facilities, but the middle and upper-socioeconomic strata possess better resources to effectuate their opposition.'

The poor should be targeted, in other words, not because they will not fight, but because, being poor, they will not win. The struggle for environmental justice is the struggle to prove that wrong.

So we start with the non-totality of the 'we'. From there not only can we see the task but we can return to our utopias, to better honour the best of them.

Those rivers of milk and wine can stop being surplus. There's nothing foolish about such yearnings: they are glimmerings in eyes set on human freedom, a leap from necessity. Far from being merely outlandish, these are abruptly aspects of a grounded utopia incorporating political economy, a yearning on behalf of those who strive without power. In the medieval peasant utopia Cockaigne, it rains cheese. Charles Fourier imagined the seas turned to lemonade. The Big Rock Candy Mountain. These are dreams of sustenance out of reach of the dreamers, of the reduction of labour, of a world that will let exhausted humanity rest.

We can dispense with the most banal critiques of utopia. That it is unconvincing as a blueprint, as if that is what it should ever be. That it is drab, boring, faceless and colourless and always the same. The smear that the visionary aspiration for better things always makes things worse. These canards serve stasis.

There are sharper criticisms to be made, for the sake of our utopias themselves and of the day-to-day interventions without which they risk being – and this, itself, is one of those criticisms – valves to release pressure.

Utopia, for one thing, has never been the preserve of those who cleave to liberation. Settlers and expropriators have for centuries asserted their good environmental sense against the laziness of feckless natives, in realising the potential of land spuriously designated empty, of making so-called deserts so-called bloom. Ecotopia has justified settlement and empire since long before the UN's REDD schemes. It has justified murder.

There is a vision of the world as a garden, under threat. Choked with toxic growth. Gardening as war. And the task being one of 'ruthlessly eliminating the weeds that would deprive the better plants of nutrition, the air, light, sun'.

Here the better plants are Aryans. The weeds are Jews.

SS-Obergruppenfuhrer and Reichsminister of Agriculture in the Third Reich, Walther Darré, coagulated soil science, nostalgia, pagan kitsch, imperialism, agrarian mystique and race hate in a vision of green renewal and earth stewardship predicated on genocide. He was the most powerful theorist of *Blut und Boden*, 'Blood and Soil', a Nazi ecotopia of organic farmlands and restocked Nordic forests, protected by the pure-blooded peasant-soldier.

The tree may not have grown as Darré hoped, but its roots didn't die. A whole variety of fascist groups across the world still proclaim their fidelity to ecological renewal, a green world, and agitate ostentatiously against climate change, pollution and despoliation, declaring against those poisons in the service of another, the logic of race.

Of course reactionary apologists for Big Pollute routinely slander ecological activists as fascists. That doesn't mean those committed to such activism should not be ruthless in ferreting out any real overlaps: very much the opposite.

Aspects of eliminationist bad utopia can be found much more widely than in the self-conscious Far Right. Swathes of ecological thinking are caught up with a nebulous, sentimentalised spiritualist utopia, what the ecofeminist Chaia Heller calls 'Eco-la-la'. Crossbred with crude Malthusianism, in the combative variant called Deep Ecology, the tweeness of that vision can morph into brutality, according to which the problem is overpopulation, humanity itself. At its most cheerfully eccentric lies the Voluntary Human Extinction Movement, advocating an end to breeding: at the most vicious are the pronouncements of David Foreman of Earth First!, faced with the Ethiopian famine of 1984: '[T]he worst thing we could do in Ethiopia is to give aid – the best thing would be to just let nature seek its own balance, to let the people there just starve'.

This is an ecological utopia of mass death. Which we could also call an apocalypse.

Apocalypse and utopia: the end of everything, and the horizon of hope. Far from antipodes, these two have always been inextricable.

Sometimes, as in Lactantius, the imagined relationship is chronological, even of cause and effect. The one, the apocalypse, the end-times rending of the veil, paves the way for the other, the time beyond, the new beginning.

Something has happened: now they are more intimately imbricated than ever. 'Today,' the bleak and sinister philosopher Emil Cioran announces, 'reconciled with the terrible, we are seeing a contamination of utopia by apocalypse . . . The two genres . . . which once seemed so dissimilar to us, interpenetrate, rub off on each other, to form a third.' Such reconciliation with the terrible, such interpenetration, is vivid in these Deep Ecological hankerings for a world slashed and burned of humans. The scourging has become the dream.

This is not quite a dystopia: it's a third form – apocatopia, utopalypse – and it's all around us. We're surrounded by a culture of ruination, dreams of falling cities, a peopleless world where animals explore. We know the clichés. Vines reclaim Wall Street as if it belongs to them, rather than the other way round; trash vastness, dunes of garbage; the remains of some great just-recognisable bridge now broken to jut, a portentous diving board, into the void. Etcetera.

It's as if we still hanker to see something better and beyond the rubble, but lack the strength. Or as if there's a concerted effort to assert the 'We' again, though negatively – 'We' are the problem, and thus this We-lessness a sublime solution. The melancholy is disingenuous. There's enthusiasm, a disa-vowed investment in these supposed warnings, these catas-trophes. The apocalypse-mongers fool no one. Since long before Shelley imagined the day when 'Westminster Abbey shall stand, shapeless and nameless ruins, in the midst of an unpeopled marsh', these have been scenes of beauty.

We've all scrolled slack-mouthed through images of the Chernobyl zone, of Japan's deserted Gunkanjima island, of the ruins of Detroit, through clickbait lists of Top Ten Most Awesomely Creepy Abandoned Places. This shouldn't occasion guilt. Our horror at the tragedies and crimes behind some such images is real: it coexists with, rather than effaces, our gasp of awe. We don't choose what catches our breath. Nor do the images that enthral us read off reductively to particular politics. But certainly the amoral beauty of our apocatopias can dovetail with something brutal and malefic, an eliminationist disgust.

We can't not read such camply symptomatic cultural matter diagnostically. What else can we do with the deluge of films of deluge, the piling up, like debris under Benjamin's angel of history, of texts about the piling up of debris?

Symptoms morph with the world. One swallow, of however high a budget, does not a summer make, but one doesn't have to be a subtle semiotician to diagnose a cultural shift when, in Guillermo Del Toro's recent *Pacific Rim*, Idris Elba bellows, 'Today we are cancelling the apocalypse!' Perhaps we've had our fill of the end, and with this line we usher in a different kind of aftermath – the apocalypse that fails. We're back, with muscular new hope.

A similar shift is visible in the rise of geoengineering, ideas once pulp fiction and the ruminations of eccentrics. Now, planet-scale plans to spray acid into the stratosphere to become mirrored molecules to reflect radiation, to scrub CO_2 from the atmosphere, to bring up benthic waters to cool the oceans, are written up by Nobel laureates, discussed in the *New Yorker* and the *MIT Technology Review*. A new hope, a new can-do, the return of human agency, sleeves rolled up, fixing the problem. With *Science*.

This planet-hacking, however, is utterly speculative, controversial, and – according to recent work at Germany's Helmholtz Centre – by the most generous possible projections thoroughly inadequate to halt climate chaos. It is, by any reasonable standards, absurd that such plans seem more rational than enacting the social measures to slash emissions that are entirely possible *right now*, but which would necessitate a transformation of our political system.

It's a left cliché to pronounce that these days it's easier to imagine the end of the world than the end of capitalism: Andreas Malm points out that with the trope of geoengineering, it's easier to imagine the deliberate transformation of the entire planet than of our political economy. What looks at first like a new Prometheanism is rather capitulation, surrender to the status quo. Utopia is here exoneration of entrenched power, the red lines of which are not to be crossed. What price hope indeed?

Seventy per cent of the staff at the mothballed Union Carbide factory in Bhopal, India, had been docked pay for refusing to break safety routines. Staffing levels were inadequate, readings taken half as often as intended. None of the six safety systems worked as it should, if at all. The trade union had protested, and been ignored.

On 3 December 1984, twenty-seven tonnes of methyl isocyanate spewed from the plant. Between 8,000 and 10,000 people died that night; 25,000 have died since. Half a million were injured, around 70,000 permanently and hideously. The rate of birth defects in the area is vastly high. The groundwater still shows toxins massively above safe levels.

Initially, the Indian government demanded $3.3 billion in compensation, which Union Carbide spent $50 million fighting. At last, in 1989, the company settled out of court for $470 million, 15 per cent of that initial sum. The survivors received, as lifetime compensation, between $300 and $500 each. In the words of Kathy Hunt, Dow-Carbide's public affairs officer, in 2002, '$500 is plenty good for an Indian.'

Why rehearse these terrible, familiar facts? Not only because, as is well known, Warren Anderson, Carbide's ex-CEO, has never been extradited to face Indian justice, despite an arrest warrant being issued. Nor because Carbide, and Dow Chemicals, which bought it in 2001, deny all responsibility, and refuse to clean the area or to respond to Indian court summonses. There is another reason.

In 1989, the *Wall Street Journal* reported that US executives were extremely anxious about this first major test of a US corporation's liability for an accident in the developing world. At last, in October 1991, came the key moment for this discussion: the Indian Supreme Court upheld Carbide's offer and dismissed all outstanding petitions against it, thereby offering the company legal protection. And its share price immediately spiked high. Because Wall Street knew its priorities had prevailed. That it was safe.

A real-world interpenetration of apocalypse and utopia. Apocalypse for those thousands who drowned on their own lungs. And for the corporations, now reassured that the poor, unlike profit, were indeed dispensable? An everyday utopia.

This is another of the limitations of utopia: we *live* in utopia; it just isn't ours.

So we live in apocalypse too.

Earth: to be determined. Utopia? Apocalypse? Is it worse to hope or to despair? To that question there can only be one answer: yes. It is worse to hope or to despair.

Bad hope and bad despair are mutually constitutive. Capitalism gets you coming or going. 'We' can fix the problem 'we' made. And when 'we', geoengineers, fail, 'we' can live through it, whisper 'our' survivalist bad consciences, the preppers hoarding cans of beans.

Is there a better optimism? And a right way to lose hope? It depends who's hoping, for what, for whom – and against whom. We must learn to hope with teeth.

We won't be browbeaten by demands for our own bureaucratised proposals. In fact there is no dearth of models to consider, but the radical critique of the everyday stands even in the absence of an alternative. We can go further: if we take utopia seriously, as a total reshaping, its scale means we can't think it from this side. It's the process of making it that will allow us to do so. It is utopian fidelity that might underpin our refusal to expound it, or any roadmap.

We should utopia as hard as we can. Along with a fulfilled humanity we should imagine flying islands, self-constituting coraline neighbourhoods, photosynthesizing cars bred from biospliced bone-marrow. Big Rock Candy Mountains. Because we'll never mistake those dreams for blueprints, nor for mere absurdities.

What utopias are are new Rorschachs. We pour our concerns and ideas out, and then in dreaming we fold the paper to open it again and reveal startling patterns. We may pour with a degree of intent, but what we make is beyond precise planning. Our utopias are to be enjoyed and admired: they are made of our concerns and they tell us about our now, about our pre-utopian selves. They are to be interpreted. And so are those of our enemies.

To understand what we're up against means to respect it. The Earth is not being blistered because the despoilers are stupid or irrational or making a mistake or have insufficient data. We should fight our case as urgently as we can, and win arguments, but we shouldn't fool ourselves: whatever the self-delusion, guilt, or occasional tears of a CEO, in a profit-maximizing world it's *rational* for the institutions of our status quo to do what they do. Individuals and even sometimes some organisations may resist that in specific cases, but only by refusing that system's logic. Which the system itself of course cannot do.

The fight for ecological justice means a fight against that system, because there is massive profit in injustice. This battle won't always be over catastrophic climate change or land expropriation: in neoliberalism, even local struggles for fleeting moments of green municipal life are ultimately struggles against power. The protests that shook the Turkish state in 2013 started with a government plan to build over Gezi Park, one of the last green spaces in the city.

Rather than touting togetherness, we fight best by embracing our not-togetherness. The fact that there are sides. Famously, we are approaching a tipping point. Rather than hoping for cohesion, our best hope lies in conflict. Our aim, an aspect of our utopianism, should be this strategy of tension.

There is bad pessimism as well as bad optimism. Against the curmudgeonly surrender of, say, James Lovelock, there are at least plausible scientific reasons to suggest that we're not yet – quite – at some point of no return, and in any case, even a broken world is worth fighting for. We need to tilt at a different tipping point, into irrevocable *social* change, and that requires a different pessimism, an unflinching look at how bad things are.

Pessimism has a bad rap among activists, terrified of surrender. But activism without the pessimism that rigor should provoke is just sentimentality.

There is hope. But for it to be real, and barbed, and tempered into a weapon, we cannot just default to it. We have to test it, subject it to the strain of appropriate near-despair. We need utopia, but to try to think utopia, in this

26

world, without rage, without fury, is an indulgence we can't afford. In the face of what is done, we cannot think utopia without hate.

Even our ends-of-the-world are too Whiggish. Let us put an end to one-nation apocalypse. Here instead is to antinomian utopia. A hope that abjures the hope of those in power.

It is the supposedly sensible critics who are the most profoundly unrealistic. As Joel Kovel says, 'we can have the accumulation of capital, and we can have ecological integrity, but we can't have both of them together'. To believe otherwise would be quaint were it not so dangerous.

In 2003, William Stavropoulos, CEO of Dow – who has, recall, no responsibility to the chemically maimed of Bhopal – said in a press release, 'Being environmentally responsible makes good business sense.'

And that, in the pejorative sense, is the most absurd utopia of all.

PART II:
UTOPIA

by Thomas More

Discourses of Raphael Hythloday, of the Best State of a Commonwealth

Henry VIII, the unconquered King of England, a prince adorned with all the virtues that become a great monarch, having some differences of no small consequence with Charles the most serene Prince of Castile, sent me into Flanders, as his ambassador, for treating and composing matters between them. I was colleague and companion to that incomparable man Cuthbert Tonstal, whom the King, with such universal applause, lately made Master of the Rolls; but of whom I will say nothing; not because I fear that the testimony of a friend will be suspected, but rather because his learning and virtues are too great for me to do them justice, and so well known that they need not my commendations, unless I would, according to the proverb, 'Show the sun with a lantern.'

Those that were appointed by the Prince to treat with us, met us at Bruges, according to agreement; they were all worthy men. The Margrave of Bruges was their head, and the chief man among them; but he that was esteemed the wisest, and that spoke for the rest, was George Temse, the

Provost of Casselsee: both art and nature had concurred to make him eloquent: he was very learned in the law; and, as he had a great capacity, so, by a long practice in affairs, he was very dexterous at unravelling them. After we had several times met, without coming to an agreement, they went to Brussels for some days, to know the Prince's pleasure; and, since our business would admit it, I went to Antwerp.

While I was there, among many that visited me, there was one that was more acceptable to me than any other, Peter Giles, born at Antwerp, who is a man of great honour, and of a good rank in his town, though less than he deserves; for I do not know if there be anywhere to be found a more learned and a better-bred young man; for as he is both a very worthy and a very knowing person, so he is so civil to all men, so particularly kind to his friends, and so full of candour and affection, that there is not, perhaps, above one or two anywhere to be found, that is in all respects so perfect a friend: he is extraordinarily modest, there is no artifice in him, and yet no man has more of a prudent simplicity. His conversation was so pleasant and so innocently cheerful that his company in a great measure lessened any longings to go back to my country, and to my wife and children, which an absence of four months had quickened very much.

One day, as I was returning home from mass at St Mary's, which is the chief church, and the most frequented of any in Antwerp, I saw him, by accident, talking with a stranger, who seemed past the flower of his age; his face was tanned, he had a long beard, and his cloak was hanging carelessly about him, so that, by his looks and habit, I concluded he was a seaman. As soon as Peter saw me, he came and saluted me, and as I was returning his civility, he took me aside, and pointing to him with whom he had been discoursing, he said, 'Do you see that man? I was just thinking to bring him to you.'

I answered, 'He should have been very welcome on your account.'

'And on his own too', replied he, 'if you knew the man, for there is none alive that can give so copious an account of unknown nations and countries as he can do, which I know you very much desire.'

'Then', said I, 'I did not guess amiss, for at first sight I took him for a seaman.' 'But you are much mistaken', said he, 'for he has not sailed as a seaman, but as a traveller, or rather a philosopher. This Raphael, who from his family carries the name of Hythloday, is not ignorant of the Latin tongue, but is eminently learned in the Greek, having applied himself more particularly to that than to the former, because he had given himself much to philosophy, in which he knew that the Romans have left us nothing that is valuable, except what is to be found in Seneca and Cicero. He is a Portuguese by birth, and was so desirous of seeing the world that he divided his estate among his brothers, ran the same hazard as Americus Vesputius, and bore a share in three of his four voyages that are now published; only he did not return with him in his last, but obtained leave of him, almost by force, that he might be one of those twenty-four who were left at the farthest place at which they touched in their last voyage to New Castile. The leaving him thus did not a little gratify one that was more fond of travelling than of returning home to be buried in his own country; for he used often to say that the way to heaven was the same from all places, and he that had no grave had the heavens still over him. Yet this disposition of mind had cost him dear, if God had not been very gracious to him; for after he, with five Castilians, had travelled over many countries, at last, by strange good fortune, he got to Ceylon, and from thence to Calicut, where he, very happily, found some Portuguese ships; and, beyond all men's expectations, returned to his native country.'

When Peter had said this to me, I thanked him for his kindness in intending to give me the acquaintance of a man whose conversation he knew would be so acceptable; and upon that Raphael and I embraced each other. After those civilities were past which are usual with strangers upon their first meeting, we all went to my house, and entering into the garden, sat down on a green bank and entertained one another in discourse.

He told us that when Vesputius had sailed away, he, and his companions that stayed behind in New Castile, by degrees insinuated themselves into the affections of the people of the country, meeting often with them and treating them gently; and at last they not only lived among them without danger, but conversed familiarly with them, and got so far into the heart of a prince, whose name and country I have forgot, that he both furnished them plentifully with all things necessary, and also with the conveniences of travelling, both boats when they went by water, and wagons when they trained over land: he sent with them a very faithful guide, who was to introduce and recommend them to such other princes as they had a mind to see: and after many days' journey, they came to towns, and cities, and to commonwealths, that were both happily governed and well peopled.

Under the equator, and as far on both sides of it as the sun moves, there lay vast deserts that were parched with the perpetual heat of the sun; the soil was withered, all things looked dismally, and all places were either quite uninhabited, or abounded with wild beasts and serpents, and some few men, that were neither less wild nor less cruel than the beasts themselves. But, as they went farther, a new scene opened, all things grew milder, the air less burning, the soil more verdant, and even the beasts were less wild: and, at last, there were nations, towns, and cities, that had not only mutual commerce among themselves and with their neighbours, but traded, both by sea and land, to very remote countries. There they found the conveniences of seeing many countries on all hands, for no ship went any voyage into which he and his companions were not very welcome.

The first vessels that they saw were flat-bottomed, their sails were made of reeds and wicker, woven close together, only some were of leather; but, afterwards, they found ships made with round keels and canvas sails, and in all respects like our ships, and the seamen understood both astronomy and navigation. He got wonderfully into their favour by showing them the use of the needle, of which till then they were utterly ignorant. They sailed before with great caution, and only in summer time; but now they count all seasons alike, trusting wholly to the loadstone, in which they are, perhaps, more secure than safe; so that there is reason to fear that this discovery, which was thought would prove so much to their advantage, may, by their imprudence, become an occasion of much mischief to them.

But it were too long to dwell on all that he told us he had observed in every place, it would be too great a digression from our present purpose: whatever is necessary to be told concerning those wise and prudent institutions which he observed among civilized nations, may perhaps be related by us on a more proper occasion. We asked him many questions concerning all these things, to which he answered very willingly; we made no inquiries after monsters, than which nothing is more common; for everywhere one may hear of ravenous dogs and wolves, and cruel men-eaters, but it is not so easy to find states that are well and wisely governed.

As he told us of many things that were amiss in those new-discovered countries, so he reckoned up not a few things, from which patterns might be taken for correcting the errors of these nations among whom we live; of which an account may be given, as I have already promised, at some other time; for, at present, I intend only to relate those particulars that he told us, of the manners and laws of the Utopians: but I will begin with the occasion that led us to speak of that commonwealth.

After Raphael had discoursed with great judgment on the many errors that were both among us and these nations, had treated of the wise institutions both here and there, and had spoken as distinctly of the customs and government of every nation through which he had passed, as if he had spent his whole life in it, Peter, being struck with admiration, said, 'I wonder, Raphael, how it comes that you enter into no king's service, for I am sure there are none to whom you would not be very acceptable; for your learning and knowledge, both of men and things, is such that you would not only entertain them very pleasantly, but be of great use to them, by the examples you could set before them, and the advices you could give them; and by this means you would both serve your own interest, and be of great use to all your friends.'

'As for my friends', answered he, 'I need not be much concerned, having already done for them all that was incumbent on me; for when I was not only in good health, but fresh and young, I distributed that among my kindred and friends which other people do not part with till they are old and sick: when they then unwillingly give that which they can enjoy no longer themselves. I think my friends ought to rest contented with this, and not to expect that for their sakes I should enslave myself to any king whatsoever.'

'Soft and fair!' said Peter; 'I do not mean that you should be a slave to any king, but only that you should assist them and be useful to them.'

'The change of the word', said he, 'does not alter the matter.'

'But term it as you will', replied Peter, 'I do not see any other way in which you can be so useful, both in private to your friends and to the public, and by which you can make your own condition happier.'

'Happier?' answered Raphael, 'Is that to be compassed in a way so abhorrent to my genius? Now I live as I will, to which I believe, few courtiers can pretend; and there are so many that court the favour of great men that there will be no great loss if they are not troubled either with me or with others of my temper.'

Upon this, said I, 'I perceive, Raphael, that you neither desire wealth nor greatness; and, indeed, I value and admire such a man much more than I do any of the great men in the world. Yet I think you would do what would well become so generous and philosophical a soul as yours is, if you would apply your time and thoughts to public affairs, even though you may happen to find it a little uneasy to yourself; and this you can never do with so much advantage as by being taken into the council of some great prince and putting him on noble and worthy actions, which I know you would do if you were in such a post; for the springs both of good and evil flow from the prince over a whole nation, as from a lasting fountain. So much learning as you have, even without practice in affairs, or so great a practice as you have had, without any other learning, would render you a very fit counsellor to any king whatsoever.'

'You are doubly mistaken', said he, 'Mr More, both in your opinion of me and in the judgment you make of things: for as I have not that capacity that you fancy I have, so if I had it, the public would not be one jot the better when I had sacrificed my quiet to it. For most princes apply themselves more to affairs of war than to the useful arts of peace; and in these I neither have any knowledge, nor do I much desire it; they are generally more set on acquiring new kingdoms, right or wrong, than on governing well those they possess: and, among the ministers of princes, there are none that are not so wise as to need no assistance, or at least, that do not think themselves so wise that they imagine they need none; and if they court any, it is only those for whom the prince has much personal favour, whom by their fawning and flatteries they endeavour to fix to their own interests; and, indeed, nature has so made us that we all love to be flattered and to please ourselves with our own notions: the old crow loves his young, and the ape her cubs. Now if in such a court, made up of persons who envy all others and only admire themselves, a person should but propose anything that he had either read in history or observed in his travels, the rest would think that the reputation of their wisdom would sink, and that their interests would be much depressed if they could not run it down: and, if all other things failed, then they would fly to this, that such or such things pleased our ancestors, and it were well for us if we could but match them. They would set up their rest on such an answer, as a sufficient confutation of all that could be said, as if it were a great misfortune that any should be found wiser than his ancestors. But though they willingly let go all the good things that were among those of former ages, yet, if better things are proposed, they cover themselves obstinately with this excuse of reverence to past times. I have met with these proud, morose, and absurd judgments of things in many places, particularly once in England.'

'Were you ever there?' said I.

'Yes, I was', answered he, 'and stayed some months there, not long after the rebellion in the West was suppressed, with a great slaughter of the poor people that were engaged in it. I was then much obliged to that reverend prelate, John Morton, Archbishop of Canterbury, Cardinal, and Chancellor of England; a man', said he, 'Peter (for Mr More knows well what he was), that was not less venerable for his wisdom and virtues than for the high character he bore: he was of a middle stature, not broken with age; his looks begot reverence rather than fear; his conversation was easy, but serious and grave; he sometimes took pleasure to try the force of those that came as suitors to him upon business by speaking sharply, though decently, to them, and by that he discovered their spirit and presence of mind; with which he was much delighted when it did not grow up to impudence, as bearing a great resemblance to his own temper, and he looked on such persons as the fittest men for affairs. He spoke both gracefully and weightily; he was eminently skilled in the law, had a vast understanding, and a prodigious memory; and those excellent talents with which nature had furnished him were improved by study and experience. When I was in England the King depended much on his counsels, and the Government seemed to be chiefly supported by him; for from his youth he had been all along practised in affairs; and, having passed through many traverses of fortune, he had, with great cost, acquired a vast stock of wisdom, which is not soon lost when it is purchased so dear.

'One day, when I was dining with him, there happened to be at table one of the English lawyers, who took occasion to run out in a high commendation of the severe execution of justice upon thieves, "who", as he said, "were then hanged so fast that there were sometimes twenty on one gibbet!" and, upon that, he said, "he could not wonder enough how it came to pass that, since so few escaped, there were yet so many thieves left, who were still robbing in all places".

'Upon this, I (who took the boldness to speak freely before the Cardinal) said, "There was no reason to wonder at the matter, since this way of punishing thieves was neither just in itself nor good for the public; for, as the severity was too great, so the remedy was not effectual; simple theft not being so great a crime that it ought to cost a man his life; no punishment, how severe soever, being able to restrain those from robbing who can find out no other way of livelihood. In this", said I, "not only you in England, but a great part of the world, imitate some ill masters, that are readier to chastise their scholars than to teach them. There are dreadful punishments enacted against thieves, but it were much better to make such good provisions by which every man might be put in a method how to live, and so be preserved from the fatal necessity of stealing and of dying for it."

' "There has been care enough taken for that", said he; "there are many handicrafts, and there is husbandry, by which they may make a shift to live, unless they have a greater mind to follow ill courses."

' "That will not serve your turn", said I, "for many lose their limbs in civil or foreign wars, as lately in the Cornish rebellion, and some time ago in your wars with France, who, being thus mutilated in the service of their king and country, can no more follow their old trades, and are too old to learn new ones; but since wars are only accidental things, and have intervals, let us consider those things that fall out every day. There is a great number of noblemen among you that are themselves as idle as drones, that subsist on other men's labour, on the labour of their tenants, whom, to raise their revenues, they pare to the quick. This, indeed, is the only instance of their frugality, for in all other things they are prodigal, even to the beggaring of themselves; but, besides this, they carry about with them a great number of idle fellows, who never learned any art by which they may gain their living; and these, as soon as either their lord dies, or they themselves fall sick, are turned out of doors; for your lords are readier to feed idle people than to take care of the sick; and often the heir is not able to keep together so great a family as his predecessor did. Now, when the stomachs of those that are thus turned out of doors grow keen, they rob no less keenly; and what else can they do? For when, by

wandering about, they have worn out both their health and
their clothes, and are tattered, and look ghastly, men of
quality will not entertain them, and poor men dare not do it,
knowing that one who has been bred up in idleness and
pleasure, and who was used to walk about with his sword
and buckler, despising all the neighbourhood with an insolent scorn as far below him, is not fit for the spade and
mattock; nor will he serve a poor man for so small a hire and
in so low a diet as he can afford to give him."

'To this he answered, "This sort of men ought to be
particularly cherished, for in them consists the force of the
armies for which we have occasion; since their birth inspires
them with a nobler sense of honour than is to be found
among tradesmen or ploughmen."

' "You may as well say", replied I, "that you must cherish
thieves on the account of wars, for you will never want the
one as long as you have the other; and as robbers prove
sometimes gallant soldiers, so soldiers often prove brave
robbers, so near an alliance there is between those two sorts
of life. But this bad custom, so common among you, of keeping many servants, is not peculiar to this nation. In France
there is yet a more pestiferous sort of people, for the whole
country is full of soldiers, still kept up in time of peace (if
such a state of a nation can be called a peace); and these are
kept in pay upon the same account that you plead for those
idle retainers about noblemen: this being a maxim of those
pretended statesmen, that it is necessary for the public safety
to have a good body of veteran soldiers ever in readiness.
They think raw men are not to be depended on, and they
sometimes seek occasions for making war, that they may
train up their soldiers in the art of cutting throats, or, as

Sallust observed, "for keeping their hands in use, that they may not grow dull by too long an intermission." But France has learned to its cost how dangerous it is to feed such beasts. The fate of the Romans, Carthaginians, and Syrians, and many other nations and cities, which were both overturned and quite ruined by those standing armies, should make others wiser; and the folly of this maxim of the French appears plainly even from this, that their trained soldiers often find your raw men prove too hard for them, of which I will not say much, lest you may think I flatter the English. Every day's experience shows that the mechanics in the towns or the clowns in the country are not afraid of fighting with those idle gentlemen, if they are not disabled by some misfortune in their body or dispirited by extreme want; so that you need not fear that those well-shaped and strong men (for it is only such that noblemen love to keep about them till they spoil them), who now grow feeble with ease and are softened with their effeminate manner of life, would be less fit for action if they were well bred and well employed. And it seems very unreasonable that, for the prospect of a war, which you need never have but when you please, you should maintain so many idle men, as will always disturb you in time of peace, which is ever to be more considered than war. But I do not think that this necessity of stealing arises only from hence; there is another cause of it, more peculiar to England."

' "What is that?" said the Cardinal.

' "The increase of pasture", said I, "by which your sheep, which are naturally mild, and easily kept in order, may be said now to devour men and unpeople, not only villages, but towns; for wherever it is found that the sheep of any soil yield a softer and richer wool than ordinary, there the nobility and gentry, and even those holy men – the abbots! – not contented with the old rents which their farms yielded, nor thinking it enough that they, living at their ease, do no good to the public, resolve to do it hurt instead of good. They stop the course of agriculture, destroying houses and towns, reserving only the churches, and enclose grounds that they may lodge their sheep in them. As if forests and parks had swallowed up too little of the land, those worthy countrymen turn the best inhabited places into solitudes; for when an insatiable wretch, who is a plague to his country, resolves to enclose many thousand acres of ground, the owners, as well as tenants, are turned out of their possessions by trick or by main force, or, being wearied out by ill usage, they are forced to sell them; by which means those miserable people, both men and women, married and unmarried, old and young, with their poor but numerous families (since country business requires many hands), are all forced to change their seats, not knowing whither to go; and they must sell, almost for nothing, their household stuff, which could not bring them much money, even though they might stay for a buyer. When that little money is at an end (for it will be soon spent), what is left for them to do but either to steal, and so to be hanged (God knows how justly!), or to go about and beg? And if they do this they are put in prison as idle vagabonds, while they would willingly work but can find none that will hire them; for there is no more occasion for country labour, to which they have been bred, when there is no arable ground left. One shepherd can look after a flock, which will stock an extent of ground that would require many hands if it were to be ploughed and reaped.

' "This, likewise, in many places raises the price of corn. The price of wool is also so risen that the poor people, who were wont to make cloth, are no more able to buy it; and this, likewise, makes many of them idle: for since the increase of pasture God has punished the avarice of the owners by a rot among the sheep, which has destroyed vast numbers of them – to us it might have seemed more just had it fell on the owners themselves. But, suppose the sheep should increase ever so much, their price is not likely to fall; since, though they cannot be called a monopoly, because they are not engrossed by one person, yet they are in so few hands, and these are so rich, that, as they are not pressed to sell them sooner than they have a mind to it, so they never do it till they have raised the price as high as possible.

' "And on the same account it is that the other kinds of cattle are so dear, because many villages being pulled down, and all country labour being much neglected, there are none who make it their business to breed them. The rich do not breed cattle as they do sheep, but buy them lean and at low prices; and, after they have fattened them on their grounds, sell them again at high rates. And I do not think that all the inconveniences this will produce are yet observed; for, as they sell the cattle dear, so, if they are consumed faster than the breeding countries from which they are brought can afford them, then the stock must decrease, and this must needs end in great scarcity; and by these means, this your island, which seemed as to this particular the happiest in the world, will suffer much by the cursed avarice of a few persons: besides this, the rising of corn makes all people lessen their families as much as they can; and what can those who are dismissed by them do but either beg or rob? And to this last a man of a great mind is much sooner drawn than to the former.

'"Luxury likewise breaks in apace upon you to set forward your poverty and misery; there is an excessive vanity in apparel, and great cost in diet, and that not only in noblemen's families, but even among tradesmen, among the farmers themselves, and among all ranks of persons. You have also many infamous houses, and, besides those that are known, the taverns and ale-houses are no better; add to these dice, cards, tables, football, tennis, and quoits, in which money runs fast away; and those that are initiated into them must, in the conclusion, betake themselves to robbing for a supply. Banish these plagues, and give orders that those who have dispeopled so much soil may either rebuild the villages they have pulled down or let out their grounds to such as will do it; restrain those engrossings of the rich that are as bad almost as monopolies; leave fewer occasions to idleness; let agriculture be set up again, and the manufacture of the wool be regulated, that so there may be work found for those companies of idle people whom want forces to be thieves, or who now, being idle vagabonds or useless servants, will certainly grow thieves at last. If you do not find a remedy to these evils it is a vain thing to boast of your severity in punishing theft, which, though it may have the appearance of justice, yet in itself is neither just nor convenient; for if you suffer your people to be ill-educated, and their manners to be corrupted from their infancy, and then punish them for those crimes to which their first education disposed them, what else is to be concluded from this but that you first make thieves and then punish them?"

'While I was talking thus, the Counsellor, who was present, had prepared an answer, and had resolved to resume all I had said, according to the formality of a debate, in which things are generally repeated more faithfully than they are answered, as if the chief trial to be made were of men's memories.

' "You have talked prettily, for a stranger", said he, "having heard of many things among us which you have not been able to consider well; but I will make the whole matter plain to you, and will first repeat in order all that you have said; then I will show how much your ignorance of our affairs has misled you; and will, in the last place, answer all your arguments. And, that I may begin where I promised, there were four things – "

' "Hold your peace!" said the Cardinal; "this will take up too much time; therefore we will, at present, ease you of the trouble of answering, and reserve it to our next meeting, which shall be to-morrow, if Raphael's affairs and yours can admit of it. But, Raphael", said he to me, "I would gladly know upon what reason it is that you think theft ought not to be punished by death: would you give way to it? Or do you propose any other punishment that will be more useful to the public? For, since death does not restrain theft, if men thought their lives would be safe, what fear or force could restrain ill men? On the contrary, they would look on the mitigation of the punishment as an invitation to commit more crimes."

'I answered, "It seems to me a very unjust thing to take away a man's life for a little money, for nothing in the world can be of equal value with a man's life: and if it be said, 'that it is not for the money that one suffers, but for his breaking the law', I must say, extreme justice is an extreme injury: for

47

we ought not to approve of those terrible laws that make the smallest offences capital, nor of that opinion of the Stoics that makes all crimes equal; as if there were no difference to be made between the killing a man and the taking his purse, between which, if we examine things impartially, there is no likeness nor proportion. God has commanded us not to kill, and shall we kill so easily for a little money? But if one shall say, that by that law we are only forbid to kill any except when the laws of the land allow of it, upon the same grounds, laws may be made, in some cases, to allow of adultery and perjury: for God having taken from us the right of disposing either of our own or of other people's lives, if it is pretended that the mutual consent of men in making laws can authorize man-slaughter in cases in which God has given us no example, that it frees people from the obligation of the divine law, and so makes murder a lawful action, what is this, but to give a preference to human laws before the divine? And, if this is once admitted, by the same rule men may, in all other things, put what restrictions they please upon the laws of God. If, by the Mosaical law, though it was rough and severe, as being a yoke laid on an obstinate and servile nation, men were only fined, and not put to death for theft, we cannot imagine, that in this new law of mercy, in which God treats us with the tenderness of a father, He has given us a greater licence to cruelty than He did to the Jews.

' "Upon these reasons it is, that I think putting thieves to death is not lawful; and it is plain and obvious that it is absurd and of ill consequence to the commonwealth that a thief and a murderer should be equally punished; for if a robber sees that his danger is the same if he is convicted of theft as if he were guilty of murder, this will naturally incite him to kill the person whom otherwise he would only have robbed; since, if the punishment is the same, there is more security, and less danger of discovery, when he that can best make it is put out of the way; so that terrifying thieves too much provokes them to cruelty.

'But as to the question, "What more convenient way of punishment can be found?" I think it much easier to find out that than to invent anything that is worse; why should we doubt but the way that was so long in use among the old Romans, who understood so well the arts of government, was very proper for their punishment? They condemned such as they found guilty of great crimes to work their whole lives in quarries, or to dig in mines with chains about them. But the method that I liked best was that which I observed in my travels in Persia, among the Polylerits, who are a considerable and well-governed people: they pay a yearly tribute to the King of Persia, but in all other respects they are a free nation, and governed by their own laws: they lie far from the sea, and are environed with hills; and, being contented with the productions of their own country, which is very fruitful, they have little commerce with any other nation; and as they, according to the genius of their country, have no inclination to enlarge their borders, so their mountains and the pension they pay to the Persian, secure them from all invasions. Thus they have no wars among them; they live rather conveniently than with splendour, and may be rather called a happy nation than either eminent or famous; for I do not think that they are known, so much as by name, to any but their next neighbours.

'Those that are found guilty of theft among them are bound to make restitution to the owner, and not, as it is in other places, to the prince, for they reckon that the prince has no more right to the stolen goods than the thief; but if that which was stolen is no more in being, then the goods of the thieves are estimated, and restitution being made out of them, the remainder is given to their wives and children; and they themselves are condemned to serve in the public works, but are neither imprisoned nor chained, unless there happens to be some extraordinary circumstance in their crimes. They go about loose and free, working for the public: if they are idle or backward to work they are whipped, but if they work hard they are well used and treated without any mark of reproach; only the lists of them are called always at night, and then they are shut up. They suffer no other uneasiness but this of constant labour; for, as they work for the public, so they are well entertained out of the public stock, which is done differently in different places: in some places whatever is bestowed on them is raised by a charitable contribution; and, though this way may seem uncertain, yet so merciful are the inclinations of that people, that they are plentifully supplied by it; but in other places public revenues are set aside for them, or there is a constant tax or poll-money raised for their maintenance. In some places they are set to no public work, but every private man that has occasion to hire workmen goes to the market-places and hires them of the public, a little lower than he would do a freeman. If they go lazily about their task he may quicken them with the whip. By this means there is always some piece of work or other to be done by them; and, besides their livelihood, they earn somewhat still to the public.

'They all wear a peculiar habit, of one certain colour, and their hair is cropped a little above their ears, and a piece of one of their ears is cut off. Their friends are allowed to give them either meat, drink, or clothes, so they are of their proper colour; but it is death, both to the giver and taker, if they give them money; nor is it less penal for any freeman to take money from them upon any account whatsoever: and it is also death for any of these slaves (so they are called) to handle arms. Those of every division of the country are distinguished by a peculiar mark, which it is capital for them to lay aside, to go out of their bounds, or to talk with a slave of another jurisdiction, and the very attempt of an escape is no less penal than an escape itself. It is death for any other slave to be accessory to it; and if a freeman engages in it he is condemned to slavery. Those that discover it are rewarded – if freemen, in money; and if slaves, with liberty, together with a pardon for being accessory to it; that so they might find their account rather in repenting of their engaging in such a design than in persisting in it.

'These are their laws and rules in relation to robbery, and it is obvious that they are as advantageous as they are mild and gentle; since vice is not only destroyed and men preserved, but they are treated in such a manner as to make them see the necessity of being honest and of employing the rest of their lives in repairing the injuries they had formerly done to society. Nor is there any hazard of their falling back to their old customs; and so little do travellers apprehend mischief from them that they generally make use of them for guides from one jurisdiction to another; for there is nothing left them by which they can rob or be the better for it, since, as they are disarmed, so the very having of money is a sufficient conviction: and as they are certainly punished if discovered, so they cannot hope to escape; for their habit being in all the parts of it different from what is commonly worn, they cannot fly away, unless they would go naked, and even then their cropped ear would betray them. The only danger to be feared from them is their conspiring against the government; but those of one division and neighbourhood can do nothing to any purpose unless a general conspiracy were laid amongst all the slaves of the several jurisdictions, which cannot be done, since they cannot meet or talk together; nor will any venture on a design where the concealment would be so dangerous and the discovery so profitable. None are quite hopeless of recovering their freedom, since by their obedience and patience, and by giving good grounds to believe that they will change their manner of life for the future, they may expect at last to obtain their liberty, and some are every year restored to it upon the good character that is given of them.

'When I had related all this, I added that I did not see why such a method might not be followed with more advantage than could ever be expected from that severe justice which the Counsellor magnified so much. To this he answered, "That it could never take place in England without endangering the whole nation."

'As he said this he shook his head, made some grimaces, and held his peace, while all the company seemed of his opinion, except the Cardinal, who said, "That it was not easy to form a judgment of its success, since it was a method that never yet had been tried; but if", said he, "when sentence of death were passed upon a thief, the prince would reprieve him for a while, and make the experiment upon him, denying him the privilege of a sanctuary; and then, if it had a good effect upon him, it might take place; and, if it did not succeed, the worst would be to execute the sentence on the condemned persons at last; and I do not see", added he, "why it would be either unjust, inconvenient, or at all dangerous to admit of such a delay; in my opinion the vagabonds ought to be treated in the same manner, against whom, though we have made many laws, yet we have not been able to gain our end."

'When the Cardinal had done, they all commended the motion, though they had despised it when it came from me, but more particularly commended what related to the vagabonds, because it was his own observation.

'I do not know whether it be worthwhile to tell what followed, for it was very ridiculous; but I shall venture at it, for as it is not foreign to this matter, so some good use may be made of it. There was a Jester standing by, that counterfeited the fool so naturally that he seemed to be really one; the jests which he offered were so cold and dull that we laughed more at him than at them, yet sometimes he said, as it were by chance, things that were not unpleasant, so as to justify the old proverb, "That he who throws the dice often, will sometimes have a lucky hit."

'When one of the company had said that I had taken care of the thieves, and the Cardinal had taken care of the vagabonds, so that there remained nothing but that some public provision might be made for the poor whom sickness or old age had disabled from labour, "Leave that to me", said the Fool, "and I shall take care of them, for there is no sort of people whose sight I abhor more, having been so often vexed with them and with their sad complaints; but as dolefully soever as they have told their tale, they could never prevail so far as to draw one penny from me; for either I had no mind to give them anything, or, when I had a mind to do it, I had nothing to give them; and they now know me so well that they will not lose their labour, but let me pass without giving me any trouble, because they hope for nothing – no more, in faith, than if I were a priest; but I would have a law made for sending all these beggars to monasteries, the men to the Benedictines, to be made lay-brothers, and the women to be nuns."

'The Cardinal smiled, and approved of it in jest, but the rest liked it in earnest. There was a divine present, who, though he was a grave morose man, yet he was so pleased with this reflection that was made on the priests and the monks that he began to play with the Fool, and said to him, "This will not deliver you from all beggars, except you take care of us Friars." "That is done already", answered the Fool, "for the Cardinal has provided for you by what he proposed for restraining vagabonds and setting them to work, for I know no vagabonds like you."

'This was well entertained by the whole company, who, looking at the Cardinal, perceived that he was not ill-pleased at it; only the Friar himself was vexed, as may be easily imagined, and fell into such a passion that he could not forbear railing at the Fool, and calling him knave, slanderer, backbiter, and son of perdition, and then cited some dreadful threatenings out of the Scriptures against him. Now the Jester thought he was in his element, and laid about him freely. "Good Friar", said he, "be not angry, for it is written, 'In patience possess your soul.'"

'The Friar answered (for I shall give you his own words), "I am not angry, you hangman; at least, I do not sin in it, for the Psalmist says, 'Be ye angry and sin not.'" Upon this the

Cardinal admonished him gently, and wished him to govern his passions. "No, my lord," said he, "I speak not but from a good zeal, which I ought to have, for holy men have had a good zeal, as it is said, 'The zeal of thy house hath eaten me up'; and we sing in our church that those who mocked Elisha as he went up to the house of God felt the effects of his zeal, which that mocker, that rogue, that scoundrel, will perhaps feel."

' "You do this, perhaps, with a good intention," said the Cardinal, "but, in my opinion, it were wiser in you, and perhaps better for you, not to engage in so ridiculous a contest with a Fool."

' "No, my lord," answered he, "that were not wisely done, for Solomon, the wisest of men, said, 'Answer a Fool according to his folly', which I now do, and show him the ditch into which he will fall, if he is not aware of it; for if the many mockers of Elisha, who was but one bald man, felt the effect of his zeal, what will become of the mocker of so many Friars, among whom there are so many bald men? We have, likewise, a bull, by which all that jeer us are excommunicated."

'When the Cardinal saw that there was no end of this matter he made a sign to the Fool to withdraw, turned the discourse another way, and soon after rose from the table, and, dismissing us, went to hear causes.

'Thus, Mr More, I have run out into a tedious story, of the length of which I had been ashamed, if (as you earnestly begged it of me) I had not observed you to hearken to it as if you had no mind to lose any part of it. I might have contracted it, but I resolved to give it you at large, that you might observe how those that despised what I had proposed, no sooner perceived that the Cardinal did not dislike it but presently approved of it, fawned so on him and flattered him to such a degree, that they in good earnest applauded those things that he only liked in jest; and from hence you may gather how little courtiers would value either me or my counsels.'

To this I answered, 'You have done me a great kindness in this relation; for as everything has been related by you both wisely and pleasantly, so you have made me imagine that I was in my own country and grown young again, by recalling that good Cardinal to my thoughts, in whose family I was bred from my childhood; and though you are, upon other accounts, very dear to me, yet you are the dearer because you honour his memory so much; but, after all this, I cannot change my opinion, for I still think that if you could overcome that aversion which you have to the courts of princes, you might, by the advice which it is in your power to give, do a great deal of good to mankind, and this is the chief design that every good man ought to propose to himself in living; for your friend Plato thinks that nations will be happy when either philosophers become kings or kings become philosophers. It is no wonder if we are so far from that happiness while philosophers will not think it their duty to assist kings with their counsels.'

'They are not so base-minded,' said he, 'but that they would willingly do it; many of them have already done it by their books, if those that are in power would but hearken to their good advice. But Plato judged right, that except kings themselves became philosophers, they who from their childhood are corrupted with false notions would never fall in entirely with the counsels of philosophers, and this he himself found to be true in the person of Dionysius.

'Do not you think that if I were about any king, proposing good laws to him, and endeavouring to root out all the
cursed seeds of evil that I found in him, I should either be
turned out of his court, or, at least, be laughed at for my
pains? For instance, what could I signify if I were about the
King of France, and were called into his cabinet council,
where several wise men, in his hearing, were proposing
many expedients; as, by what arts and practices Milan may
be kept, and Naples, that has so often slipped out of their
hands, recovered; how the Venetians, and after them the rest
of Italy, may be subdued; and then how Flanders, Brabant,
and all Burgundy, and some other kingdoms which he has
swallowed already in his designs, may be added to his
empire? One proposes a league with the Venetians, to be
kept as long as he finds his account in it, and that he ought to
communicate counsels with them, and give them some share
of the spoil till his success makes him need or fear them less,
and then it will be easily taken out of their hands; another
proposes the hiring the Germans and the securing the
Switzers by pensions; another proposes the gaining the
Emperor by money, which is omnipotent with him; another
proposes a peace with the King of Arragon, and, in order to
cement it, the yielding up the King of Navarre's pretensions;
another thinks that the Prince of Castile is to be wrought on
by the hope of an alliance, and that some of his courtiers are
to be gained to the French faction by pensions. The hardest
point of all is, what to do with England; a treaty of peace is
to be set on foot, and, if their alliance is not to be depended
on, yet it is to be made as firm as possible, and they are to be
called friends, but suspected as enemies: therefore the Scots
are to be kept in readiness to be let loose upon England on

every occasion; and some banished nobleman is to be supported underhand (for by the League it cannot be done avowedly) who has a pretension to the crown, by which means that suspected prince may be kept in awe.

'Now when things are in so great a fermentation, and so many gallant men are joining counsels how to carry on the war, if so mean a man as I should stand up and wish them to change all their counsels – to let Italy alone and stay at home, since the kingdom of France was indeed greater than could be well governed by one man; that therefore he ought not to think of adding others to it; and if, after this, I should propose to them the resolutions of the Achorians, a people that lie on the south-east of Utopia, who long ago engaged in war in order to add to the dominions of their prince another kingdom, to which he had some pretensions by an ancient alliance: this they conquered, but found that the trouble of keeping it was equal to that by which it was gained; that the conquered people were always either in rebellion or exposed to foreign invasions, while they were obliged to be incessantly at war, either for or against them, and consequently could never disband their army; that in the meantime they were oppressed with taxes, their money went out of the kingdom, their blood was spilt for the glory of their king without procuring the least advantage to the people, who received not the smallest benefit from it even in time of peace; and that, their manners being corrupted by a long war, robbery and murders everywhere abounded, and their laws fell into contempt; while their king, distracted with the care of two kingdoms, was the less able to apply his mind to the interest of either. When they saw this, and that there would be no end to these evils, they by joint counsels made an humble address to their king, desiring him to choose which of the two kingdoms he had the greatest mind to keep, since he could not hold both; for they were too great a people to be governed by a divided king, since no man would willingly have a groom that should be in common between him and another. Upon which the good prince was forced to quit his new kingdom to one of his friends (who was not long after dethroned), and to be contented with his old one. To this I would add that after all those warlike attempts, the vast confusions, and the consumption both of treasure and of people that must follow them, perhaps upon some misfortune they might be forced to throw up all at last; therefore it seemed much more eligible that the king should improve his ancient kingdom all he could, and make it flourish as much as possible; that he should love his people, and be beloved of them; that he should live among them, govern them gently and let other kingdoms alone, since that which had fallen to his share was big enough, if not too big, for him: pray, how do you think would such a speech as this be heard?'

'I confess', said I, 'I think not very well.'

'But what', said he, 'if I should sort with another kind of ministers, whose chief contrivances and consultations were by what art the prince's treasures might be increased? Where one proposes raising the value of specie when the king's debts are large, and lowering it when his revenues were to come in, that so he might both pay much with a little, and in a little receive a great deal.

'Another proposes a pretence of a war, that money might be raised in order to carry it on, and that a peace be concluded as soon as that was done; and this with such appearances of religion as might work on the people, and make them impute

it to the piety of their prince, and to his tenderness for the
lives of his subjects. A third offers some old musty laws that
have been antiquated by a long disuse (and which, as they
had been forgotten by all the subjects, so they had also been
broken by them), and proposes the levying the penalties of
these laws, that, as it would bring in a vast treasure, so there
might be a very good pretence for it, since it would look like
the executing a law and the doing of justice. A fourth
proposes the prohibiting of many things under severe penalties, especially such as were against the interest of the people,
and then the dispensing with these prohibitions, upon great
compositions, to those who might find their advantage in
breaking them. This would serve two ends, both of them
acceptable to many; for as those whose avarice led them to
transgress would be severely fined, so the selling licences
dear would look as if a prince were tender of his people, and
would not easily, or at low rates, dispense with anything that
might be against the public good. Another proposes that the
judges must be made sure, that they may declare always in
favour of the prerogative; that they must be often sent for to
court, that the king may hear them argue those points in
which he is concerned; since, how unjust soever any of his
pretensions may be, yet still some one or other of them,
either out of contradiction to others, or the pride of singu-
larity, or to make their court, would find out some pretence
or other to give the king a fair colour to carry the point. For
if the judges but differ in opinion, the clearest thing in the
world is made by that means disputable, and truth being
once brought in question, the king may then take advantage
to expound the law for his own profit; while the judges that
stand out will be brought over, either through fear or

modesty; and they being thus gained, all of them may be sent to the bench to give sentence boldly as the king would have it; for fair pretences will never be wanting when sentence is to be given in the prince's favour. It will either be said that equity lies of his side, or some words in the law will be found sounding that way, or some forced sense will be put on them; and, when all other things fail, the king's undoubted prerogative will be pretended, as that which is above all law, and to which a religious judge ought to have a special regard.

'Thus all consent to that maxim of Crassus, that a prince cannot have treasure enough, since he must maintain his armies out of it; that a king, even though he would, can do nothing unjustly; that all property is in him, not excepting the very persons of his subjects; and that no man has any other property but that which the king, out of his goodness, thinks fit to leave him. And they think it is the prince's interest that there be as little of this left as may be, as if it were his advantage that his people should have neither riches nor liberty, since these things make them less easy and willing to submit to a cruel and unjust government. Whereas necessity and poverty blunts them, makes them patient, beats them down, and breaks that height of spirit that might otherwise dispose them to rebel.

'Now what if, after all these propositions were made, I should rise up and assert that such counsels were both unbecoming a king and mischievous to him; and that not only his honour, but his safety, consisted more in his people's wealth than in his own; if I should show that they choose a king for their own sake, and not for his; that, by his care and endeavours, they may be both easy and safe; and that, therefore, a prince ought to take more care of his people's happiness than of his own, as a shepherd is to take more care of his flock than of himself?

'It is also certain that they are much mistaken that think the poverty of a nation is a mean of the public safety. Who quarrel more than beggars? Who does more earnestly long for a change than he that is uneasy in his present circumstances? And who run to create confusions with so desperate a boldness as those who, having nothing to lose, hope to gain by them? If a king should fall under such contempt or envy that he could not keep his subjects in their duty but by oppression and ill usage, and by rendering them poor and miserable, it were certainly better for him to quit his kingdom than to retain it by such methods as make him, while he keeps the name of authority, lose the majesty due to it. Nor is it so becoming the dignity of a king to reign over beggars as over rich and happy subjects.

'And therefore Fabricius, a man of a noble and exalted temper, said 'he would rather govern rich men than be rich himself; since for one man to abound in wealth and pleasure when all about him are mourning and groaning, is to be a jailer and not a king.' He is an unskilful physician that cannot cure one disease without casting his patient into another. So he that can find no other way for correcting the errors of his people but by taking from them the conveniences of life, shows that he knows not what it is to govern a free nation. He himself ought rather to shake off his sloth, or to lay down his pride, for the contempt or hatred that his people have for him takes its rise from the vices in himself. Let him live upon what belongs to him without wronging others, and accommodate his expense to his revenue. Let him punish crimes, and, by his wise conduct, let him endeavour to prevent them, rather than be severe when he has suffered them to be too common. Let him not rashly revive laws that are abrogated by disuse, especially if they have been long forgotten and never wanted. And let him never take any penalty for the breach of them to which a judge would not give way in a private man, but would look on him as a crafty and unjust person for pretending to it.

'To these things I would add that law among the Macarians – a people that live not far from Utopia – by which their king, on the day on which he began to reign, is tied by an oath, confirmed by solemn sacrifices, never to have at once above a thousand pounds of gold in his treasures, or so much silver as is equal to that in value. This law, they tell us, was made by an excellent king who had more regard to the riches of his country than to his own wealth, and therefore provided against the heaping up of so much treasure as might impoverish the people. He thought that moderate sum might be sufficient for any accident, if either the king had occasion for it against the rebels, or the kingdom against the invasion of an enemy; but that it was not enough to encourage a prince to invade other men's rights – a circumstance that was the chief cause of his making that law. He also thought that it was a good provision for that free circulation of money so necessary for the course of commerce and exchange. And when a king must distribute all those extraordinary accessions that increase treasure beyond the due pitch, it makes him less disposed to oppress his subjects. Such a king as this will be the terror of ill men, and will be beloved by all the good.

'If, I say, I should talk of these or such-like things to men that had taken their bias another way, how deaf would they be to all I could say!'

'No doubt, very deaf', answered I; 'and no wonder, for one is never to offer propositions or advice that we are certain will not be entertained. Discourses so much out of the road could not avail anything, nor have any effect on men whose minds were prepossessed with different sentiments. This philosophical way of speculation is not unpleasant among friends in a free conversation; but there is no room for it in the courts of princes, where great affairs are carried on by authority.'

'That is what I was saying', replied he, 'that there is no room for philosophy in the courts of princes.'

'Yes, there is', said I, 'but not for this speculative philosophy, that makes everything to be alike fitting at all times; but there is another philosophy that is more pliable, that knows its proper scene, accommodates itself to it, and teaches a man with propriety and decency to act that part which has fallen to his share. If when one of Plautus' comedies is upon the stage, and a company of servants are acting their parts, you should come out in the garb of a philosopher, and repeat, out of *Octavia*, a discourse of Seneca's to Nero, would it not be better for you to say nothing than by mixing things of such different natures to make an impertinent tragi-comedy? For you spoil and corrupt the play that is in hand when you mix with it things of an opposite nature, even though they are much better. Therefore go through with the play that is acting the best you can, and do not confound it because another that is pleasanter comes into your thoughts.

'It is even so in a commonwealth and in the councils of princes; if ill opinions cannot be quite rooted out, and you cannot cure some received vice according to your wishes, you must not, therefore, abandon the commonwealth, for the same reasons as you should not forsake the ship in a storm because you cannot command the winds. You are not obliged to assault people with discourses that are out of their road, when you see that their received notions must prevent your making an impression upon them: you ought rather to cast about and to manage things with all the dexterity in your power, so that, if you are not able to make them go well, they may be as little ill as possible; for, except all men were good, everything cannot be right, and that is a blessing that I do not at present hope to see.'

'According to your argument', answered he, 'all that I could be able to do would be to preserve myself from being mad while I endeavoured to cure the madness of others; for, if I speak with, I must repeat what I have said to you; and as for lying, whether a philosopher can do it or not I cannot tell: I am sure I cannot do it.

'But though these discourses may be uneasy and ungrateful to them, I do not see why they should seem foolish or extravagant; indeed, if I should either propose such things as Plato has contrived in his 'Commonwealth', or as the Utopians practise in theirs, though they might seem better, as certainly they are, yet they are so different from our establishment, which is founded on property (there being no such thing among them), that I could not expect that it would have any effect on them. But such discourses as mine, which only call past evils to mind and give warning of what may follow, leave nothing in them that is so absurd that they may not be used at any time, for they can only be unpleasant to those who are resolved to run headlong the contrary way; and if we must let alone everything as absurd or extravagant – which, by reason of the wicked lives of many, may seem uncouth – we must, even among Christians, give over pressing the greatest part of those things that Christ hath taught us, though He has commanded us not to conceal them, but to proclaim on the housetops that which He taught in secret. The greatest parts of His precepts are more opposite to the lives of the men of this age than any part of my discourse has been, but the preachers seem to have learned that craft to which you advise me: for they, observing that the world would not willingly suit their lives to the rules that Christ has given, have fitted His doctrine, as if it had been a leaden rule, to their lives, that so, some way or other, they might agree with one another.

'But I see no other effect of this compliance except it be that men become more secure in their wickedness by it; and this is all the success that I can have in a court, for I must always differ from the rest, and then I shall signify nothing; or, if I agree with them, I shall then only help forward their madness. I do not comprehend what you mean by your 'casting about', or by 'the bending and handling things so dexterously that, if they go not well, they may go as little ill as may be;' for in courts they will not bear with a man's holding his peace or conniving at what others do: a man must barefacedly approve of the worst counsels and consent to the blackest designs, so that he would pass for a spy, or, possibly, for a traitor, that did but coldly approve of such wicked practices; and therefore when a man is engaged in such a society, he will be so far from being able to mend matters by his 'casting about', as you call it, that he will find no occasions of doing any good – the ill company will sooner corrupt him than be the better for him; or if, notwithstanding all their ill company, he still remains steady and innocent, yet their follies and knavery will be imputed to him; and, by mixing counsels with them, he must bear his share of all the blame that belongs wholly to others.

'It was no ill simile by which Plato set forth the unreasonableness of a philosopher's meddling with government. "If a man", says he, "were to see a great company run out every day into the rain and take delight in being wet – if he knew that it would be to no purpose for him to go and persuade them to return to their houses in order to avoid the storm, and that all that could be expected by his going to speak to them would be that he himself should be as wet as they, it would be best for him to keep within doors, and, since he had not influence enough to correct other people's folly, to take care to preserve himself."

'Though, to speak plainly my real sentiments, I must freely own that as long as there is any property, and while money is the standard of all other things, I cannot think that a nation can be governed either justly or happily: not justly, because the best things will fall to the share of the worst men; nor happily, because all things will be divided among a few (and even these are not in all respects happy), the rest being left to be absolutely miserable.

'Therefore, when I reflect on the wise and good constitution of the Utopians, among whom all things are so well governed and with so few laws, where virtue hath its due reward, and yet there is such an equality that every man lives in plenty – when I compare with them so many other nations that are still making new laws, and yet can never bring their constitution to a right regulation; where, notwithstanding every one has his property, yet all the laws that they can invent have not the power either to obtain or preserve it, or even to enable men certainly to distinguish what is their own from what is another's, of which the many lawsuits that every day break out, and are eternally depending, give too plain a demonstration – when, I say, I balance all these things in my thoughts, I grow more favourable to Plato, and do not wonder that he resolved not to make any laws for such as would not submit to a community of all things; for so wise a man could not but foresee that the setting all upon a level was the only way to make a nation happy; which cannot be obtained so long as there is property, for when every man draws to himself all that he can encompass, by one title or another, it must needs follow that, how plentiful soever a nation may be, yet a few dividing the wealth of it among themselves, the rest must fall into indigence. So that there will be two sorts of people among them, who deserve that their fortunes should be interchanged – the former useless, but wicked and ravenous; and the latter, who by their constant industry serve the public more than themselves, sincere and modest men – from whence I am persuaded that till property is taken away, there can be no equitable or just distribution of things, nor can the world be happily governed; for as long as that is maintained, the greatest and the far best part of mankind, will be still oppressed with a load of cares and anxieties. I confess, without taking it quite away, those pressures that lie on a great part of mankind may be made lighter, but they can never be quite removed; for if laws were made to determine at how great an extent in soil, and at how much money, every man must stop – to limit the prince, that he might not grow too great; and to restrain the people, that they might not become too insolent – and that none might factiously aspire to public employments, which ought neither to be sold nor made burdensome by a great expense, since otherwise those that serve in them would be tempted to reimburse themselves by cheats and violence, and it would become necessary to find out rich men for undergoing those employments, which ought rather to be trusted to the wise. These laws, I say, might have such effect as good diet and care might have on a sick man whose recovery is desperate; they might allay and mitigate the disease, but it could never be quite healed, nor the body politic be brought again to a good habit as long as property remains; and it will fall out, as in a complication of diseases, that by applying a remedy to one sore you will provoke another, and that which removes the one ill symptom produces others, while the strengthening one part of the body weakens the rest.'

'On the contrary', answered I, 'it seems to me that men cannot live conveniently where all things are common. How can there be any plenty where every man will excuse himself from labour? For as the hope of gain doth not excite him, so the confidence that he has in other men's industry may make him slothful. If people come to be pinched with want, and yet cannot dispose of anything as their own, what can follow upon this but perpetual sedition and bloodshed, especially when the reverence and authority due to magistrates falls to the ground? For I cannot imagine how that can be kept up among those that are in all things equal to one another.'

'I do not wonder', said he, 'that it appears so to you, since you have no notion, or at least no right one, of such a constitution; but if you had been in Utopia with me, and had seen their laws and rules, as I did, for the space of five years, in which I lived among them, and during which time I was so delighted with them that indeed I should never have left them if it had not been to make the discovery of that new world to the Europeans, you would then confess that you had never seen a people so well constituted as they.'

'You will not easily persuade me', said Peter, 'that any nation in that new world is better governed than those among us; for as our understandings are not worse than theirs, so our government (if I mistake not) being more ancient, a long practice has helped us to find out many conveniences of life, and some happy chances have discovered other things to us which no man's understanding could ever have invented.'

'As for the antiquity either of their government or of ours', said he, 'you cannot pass a true judgment of it unless you had read their histories; for, if they are to be believed, they had towns among them before these parts were so much as inhabited; and as for those discoveries that have been either hit on by chance or made by ingenious men, these might have happened there as well as here. I do not deny but we are more ingenious than they are, but they exceed us much in industry and application. They knew little concerning us before our arrival among them. They call us all by a general name of "The nations that lie beyond the equinoctial line"; for their chronicle mentions a shipwreck that was made on their coast twelve hundred years ago, and that some Romans and Egyptians that were in the ship, getting safe ashore, spent the rest of their days amongst them; and such was their ingenuity that from this single opportunity they drew the advantage of learning from those unlooked-for guests, and acquired all the useful arts that were then among the Romans, and which were known to these shipwrecked men; and by the hints that they gave them they themselves found out even some of those arts which they could not fully explain, so happily did they improve that accident of having some of our people cast upon their shore. But if such an accident has at any time brought any from thence into Europe, we have been so far from improving it that we do not so much as remember it, as, in aftertimes perhaps, it will be forgot by our people that I was ever there; for though they, from one such accident, made themselves masters of all the good inventions that were among us, yet I believe it would be long before we should learn or put in practice any of the good institutions that are among them. And this is the true cause of their being better governed and living happier than we, though we come not short of them in point of understanding or outward advantages.'

Upon this I said to him, 'I earnestly beg you would describe that island very particularly to us; be not too short, but set out in order all things relating to their soil, their rivers, their towns, their people, their manners, constitution, laws, and, in a word, all that you imagine we desire to know; and you may well imagine that we desire to know everything concerning them of which we are hitherto ignorant.'

'I will do it very willingly', said he, 'for I have digested the whole matter carefully, but it will take up some time.'

'Let us go, then', said I, 'first and dine, and then we shall have leisure enough.' He consented; we went in and dined, and after dinner came back and sat down in the same place. I ordered my servants to take care that none might come and interrupt us, and both Peter and I desired Raphael to be as good as his word. When he saw that we were very intent upon it he paused a little to recollect himself, and began in this manner:

'The island of Utopia is in the middle two hundred miles broad, and holds almost at the same breadth over a great part of it, but it grows narrower towards both ends. Its figure is not unlike a crescent. Between its horns the sea comes in eleven miles broad, and spreads itself into a great bay, which is environed with land to the compass of about five hundred miles, and is well secured from winds. In this bay there is no great current; the whole coast is, as it were, one continued harbour, which gives all that live in the island great convenience for mutual commerce. But the entry into the bay, occasioned by rocks on the one hand and shallows on the other, is very dangerous. In the middle of it there is one single rock which appears above water, and may, therefore, easily be avoided; and on the top of it there is a tower, in which a garrison is kept; the other rocks lie under water, and are very dangerous. The channel is known only to the natives; so that if any stranger should enter into the bay without one of their pilots he would run great danger of shipwreck. For even they themselves could not pass it safe if some marks that are on the coast did not direct their way; and if these should be but a little shifted, any fleet that might come against them, how great soever it were, would be certainly lost.

'On the other side of the island there are likewise many harbours; and the coast is so fortified, both by nature and art, that a small number of men can hinder the descent of a great army. But they report (and there remains good marks of it to make it credible) that this was no island at first, but a part of the continent. Utopus, that conquered it (whose name it still carries, for Abraxa was its first name), brought the rude and uncivilized inhabitants into such a good government, and to that measure of politeness, that they now far excel all the rest of mankind. Having soon subdued them, he designed to separate them from the continent, and to bring the sea quite round them. To accomplish this he ordered a deep channel to be dug, fifteen miles long; and that the natives might not think he treated them like slaves, he not only forced the inhabitants, but also his own soldiers, to labour in carrying it on. As he set a vast number of men to work, he, beyond all men's expectations, brought it to a speedy conclusion. And his neighbours, who at first laughed at the folly of the undertaking, no sooner saw it brought to perfection than they were struck with admiration and terror.

'There are fifty-four cities on the island, all large and well built, the manners, customs, and laws of which are the same, and they are all contrived as near in the same manner as the ground on which they stand will allow. The nearest lie at least twenty-four miles' distance from one another, and the most remote are not so far distant but that a man can go on foot in one day from it to that which lies next it.

'Every city sends three of their wisest senators once a year to Amaurot, to consult about their common concerns; for that is the chief town of the island, being situated near the centre of it, so that it is the most convenient place for their assemblies. The jurisdiction of every city extends at least twenty miles, and, where the towns lie wider, they have much more ground. No town desires to enlarge its bounds, for the people consider themselves rather as tenants than landlords. They have built, over all the country, farmhouses for husbandmen, which are well contrived, and furnished with all things necessary for country labour. Inhabitants are sent, by turns, from the cities to dwell in them; no country family has fewer than forty men and women in it, besides two slaves. There is a master and a mistress set over every family, and over thirty families there is a magistrate. Every year twenty of this family come back to the town after they have stayed two years in the country, and in their stead there are another twenty sent from the town, that they may learn country work from those that have been already one year in the country, as they must teach those that come to them the next from the town. By this means such as dwell in those country farms are never ignorant of agriculture, and so commit no errors which might otherwise be fatal and bring them under a scarcity of corn. But though there is every year such a shifting of the husbandmen to prevent any man being forced against his will to follow that hard course of life too long, yet many among them take such pleasure in it that they desire leave to continue in it many years.

'These husbandmen till the ground, breed cattle, hew wood, and convey it to the towns either by land or water, as is most convenient. They breed an infinite multitude of chickens in a very curious manner; for the hens do not sit and hatch them, but a vast number of eggs are laid in a gentle and equal heat in order to be hatched, and they are no sooner out of the shell, and able to stir about, but they seem to consider those that feed them as their mothers, and follow them as other chickens do the hen that hatched them.

'They breed very few horses, but those they have are full of mettle, and are kept only for exercising their youth in the art of sitting and riding them; for they do not put them to any work, either of ploughing or carriage, in which they employ oxen. For though their horses are stronger, yet they find oxen can hold out longer; and as they are not subject to so many diseases, so they are kept upon a less charge and with less trouble. And even when they are so worn out that they are no more fit for labour, they are good meat at last.

'They sow no corn but that which is to be their bread; for they drink either wine, cider or perry, and often water, sometimes boiled with honey or liquorice, with which they abound; and though they know exactly how much corn will serve every town and all that tract of country which belongs to it, yet they sow much more and breed more cattle than are necessary for their consumption, and they give that surplus of which they make no use to their neighbours. When they want anything in the country which it does not produce, they fetch that from the town, without carrying anything in exchange for it. And the magistrates of the town take care to see it given them; for they meet generally in the town once a month, upon a festival day. When the time of harvest comes, the magistrates in the country send to those in the towns and let them know how many hands they will need for reaping the harvest; and the number they call for being sent to them, they commonly despatch it all in one day.

Of Their Towns, Particularly of Amaurot

'He that knows one of their towns knows them all – they are so like one another, except where the situation makes some difference. I shall therefore describe one of them, and none is so proper as Amaurot; for as none is more eminent (all the rest yielding in precedence to this, because it is the seat of their supreme council), so there was none of them better known to me, I having lived five years all together in it.

'It lies upon the side of a hill, or, rather, a rising ground. Its figure is almost square, for from the one side of it, which shoots up almost to the top of the hill, it runs down, in a descent for two miles, to the river Anider; but it is a little broader the other way that runs along by the bank of that river. The Anider rises about eighty miles above Amaurot, in a small spring at first. But other brooks falling into it, of which two are more considerable than the rest, as it runs by Amaurot it is grown half a mile broad; but, it still grows larger and larger, till, after sixty miles' course below it, it is lost in the ocean. Between the town and the sea, and for some miles above the town, it ebbs and flows every six hours with a strong current. The tide comes up about thirty miles so full that there is nothing but salt water in the river, the fresh water being driven back with its force; and above that, for some miles, the water is brackish; but a little higher, as it runs by the town, it is quite fresh; and when the tide ebbs, it continues fresh all along to the sea. There is a bridge cast over the river, not of timber, but of fair stone, consisting of many stately arches; it lies at that part of the town which is farthest from the sea, so that the ships, without any hindrance, lie all along the side of the town. There is, likewise, another river that runs by it, which, though it is not great, yet it runs pleasantly, for it rises out of the same hill on which the town stands, and so runs down through it and falls into the Anider.

'The inhabitants have fortified the fountain-head of this river, which springs a little without the towns; that so, if they should happen to be besieged, the enemy might not be able to stop or divert the course of the water, nor poison it;

from thence it is carried, in earthen pipes, to the lower streets. And for those places of the town to which the water of that small river cannot be conveyed, they have great cisterns for receiving the rain-water, which supplies the want of the other. The town is compassed with a high and thick wall, in which there are many towers and forts; there is also a broad and deep dry ditch, set thick with thorns, cast round three sides of the town, and the river is instead of a ditch on the fourth side. The streets are very convenient for all carriage, and are well sheltered from the winds. Their buildings are good, and are so uniform that a whole side of a street looks like one house. The streets are twenty feet broad; there lie gardens behind all their houses. These are large, but enclosed with buildings, that on all hands face the streets, so that every house has both a door to the street and a back door to the garden. Their doors have all two leaves, which, as they are easily opened, so they shut of their own accord; and, there being no property among them, every man may freely enter into any house whatsoever. At every ten years' end they shift their houses by lots.

'They cultivate their gardens with great care, so that they have both vines, fruits, herbs, and flowers in them; and all is so well ordered and so finely kept that I never saw gardens anywhere that were both so fruitful and so beautiful as theirs. And this humour of ordering their gardens so well is not only kept up by the pleasure they find in it, but also by an emulation between the inhabitants of the several streets, who vie with each other. And there is, indeed, nothing belonging to the whole town that is both more useful and more pleasant. So that he who founded the town seems to have taken care of nothing more than of their gardens; for they say the whole scheme of the town was designed at first by Utopus, but he left all that belonged to the ornament and improvement of it to be added by those that should come after him, that being too much for one man to bring to perfection. Their records, that contain the history of their town and State, are preserved with an exact care, and run backwards seventeen hundred and sixty years. From these it appears that their houses were at first low and mean, like cottages, made of any sort of timber, and were built with mud walls and thatched with straw.

'But now their houses are three storeys high, the fronts of them are faced either with stone, plastering, or brick, and between the facings of their walls they throw in their rubbish. Their roofs are flat, and on them they lay a sort of plaster, which costs very little, and yet is so tempered that it is not apt to take fire, and yet resists the weather more than lead. They have great quantities of glass among them, with which they glaze their windows; they use also in their windows a thin linen cloth, that is so oiled or gummed that it both keeps out the wind and gives free admission to the light.

Of Their Magistrates

'Thirty families choose every year a magistrate, who was anciently called the Syphogrant, but is now called the Philarch; and over every ten Syphogrants, with the families subject to them, there is another magistrate, who was anciently called the Tranibore, but of late the Archphilarch. All the Syphogrants, who are in number two hundred, choose the Prince out of a list of four who are named by the people of the four divisions of the city; but they take an oath, before they proceed to an election, that they will choose him whom they think most fit for the office: they give him their voices secretly, so that it is not known for whom every one gives his suffrage. The Prince is for life, unless he is removed upon suspicion of some design to enslave the people. The Tranibors are new chosen every year, but yet they are, for the most part, continued; all their other magistrates are only annual.

'The Tranibors meet every third day, and oftener if necessary, and consult with the Prince either concerning the affairs of the State in general, or such private differences as may arise sometimes among the people, though that falls out but seldom. There are always two Syphogrants called into the council chamber, and these are changed every day. It is a fundamental rule of their government, that no conclusion can be made in anything that relates to the public till it has been first debated three days in their council. It is death for any to meet and consult concerning the State, unless it be either in their ordinary council, or in the assembly of the whole body of the people.

'These things have been so provided among them that the Prince and the Tranibors may not conspire together to change the government and enslave the people; and there-fore when anything of great importance is set on foot, it is sent to the Syphogrants, who, after they have communicated it to the families that belong to their divisions, and have considered it among themselves, make report to the senate; and, upon great occasions, the matter is referred to the coun-cil of the whole island. One rule observed in their council is, never to debate a thing on the same day in which it is first proposed; for that is always referred to the next meeting, that so men may not rashly and in the heat of discourse engage themselves too soon, which might bias them so much that, instead of consulting the good of the public, they might rather study to support their first opinions, and by a perverse and preposterous sort of shame hazard their country rather than endanger their own reputation, or venture the being suspected to have wanted foresight in the expedients that they at first proposed; and therefore, to prevent this, they take care that they may rather be deliberate than sudden in their motions.

Of Their Trades, and Manner of Life

'Agriculture is that which is so universally understood among them that no person, either man or woman, is ignorant of it; they are instructed in it from their childhood, partly by what they learn at school, and partly by practice, they being led out often into the fields about the town, where they not only see others at work but are likewise exercised in it themselves.

'Besides agriculture, which is so common to them all, every man has some peculiar trade to which he applies himself; such as the manufacture of wool or flax, masonry, smith's work, or carpenter's work; for there is no sort of trade that is in great esteem among them.

'Throughout the island they wear the same sort of clothes, without any other distinction except what is necessary to distinguish the two sexes and the married and unmarried. The fashion never alters, and as it is neither disagreeable nor uneasy, so it is suited to the climate, and calculated both for their summers and winters. Every family makes their own clothes; but all among them, women as well as men, learn one or other of the trades formerly mentioned. Women, for the most part, deal in wool and flax, which suit best with their weakness, leaving the ruder trades to the men. The same trade generally passes down from father to son, inclinations often following descent: but if any man's genius lies another way he is, by adoption, translated into a family that deals in the trade to which he is inclined; and when that is to be done, care is taken, not only by his father, but by the magistrate, that he may be put to a discreet and good man: and if, after a person has learned one trade, he desires to acquire another, that is also allowed, and is managed in the same manner as the former. When he has learned both, he follows that which he likes best, unless the public has more occasion for the other.

'The chief, and almost the only, business of the Syphogrants is to take care that no man may live idle, but that every one may follow his trade diligently; yet they do not wear themselves out with perpetual toil from morning to night, as if they were beasts of burden, which as it is indeed a heavy slavery, so it is everywhere the common course of life amongst all mechanics except the Utopians: but they, dividing the day and night into twenty-four hours, appoint six of these for work, three of which are before dinner and three after; they then sup, and at eight o'clock, counting from noon, go to bed and sleep eight hours: the rest of their time, besides that taken up in work, eating, and sleeping, is left to every man's discretion; yet they are not to abuse that interval to luxury and idleness, but must employ it in some proper exercise, according to their various inclinations, which is, for the most part, reading. It is ordinary to have public lectures every morning before daybreak, at which none are obliged to appear but those who are marked out for literature; yet a great many, both men and women, of all ranks, go to hear lectures of one sort or other, according to their inclinations: but if others that are not made for contemplation, choose rather to employ themselves at that time in their trades, as many of them do, they are not hindered, but are rather commended, as men that take care to serve their country.

'After supper they spend an hour in some diversion, in summer in their gardens, and in winter in the halls where they eat, where they entertain each other either with music or discourse. They do not so much as know dice, or any such foolish and mischievous games. They have, however, two sorts of games not unlike our chess; the one is between several numbers, in which one number, as it were, consumes another; the other resembles a battle between the virtues and the vices, in which the enmity in the vices among themselves, and their agreement against virtue, is not unpleasantly represented; together with the special opposition between the particular virtues and vices; as also the methods by which vice either openly assaults or secretly undermines virtue; and virtue, on the other hand, resists it.

'But the time appointed for labour is to be narrowly examined, otherwise you may imagine that since there are only six hours appointed for work, they may fall under a scarcity of necessary provisions: but it is so far from being true that this time is not sufficient for supplying them with plenty of all things, either necessary or convenient, that it is rather too much; and this you will easily apprehend if you consider how great a part of all other nations is quite idle. First, women generally do little, who are the half of mankind; and if some few women are diligent, their husbands are idle: then consider the great company of idle priests, and of those that are called religious men; add to these all rich men, chiefly those that have estates in land, who are called noblemen and gentlemen, together with their families, made up of idle persons, that are kept more for show than use; add to these all those strong and lusty beggars that go about pretending some disease in excuse for their begging; and upon the whole account you will find that the number of those by whose labours mankind is supplied is much less than you perhaps imagined: then consider how few of those that work are employed in labours that are of real service, for we, who measure all things by money, give rise to many trades that are both vain and superfluous, and serve only to support riot and luxury: for if those who work were employed only in such things as the conveniences of life require, there would be such an abundance of them that the prices of them would so sink that tradesmen could not be maintained by their gains; if all those who labour about useless things were set to more profitable employments, and if all they that languish out their lives in sloth and idleness (every one of whom consumes as much as any two of the men that are at work) were forced to labour, you may easily imagine that a small proportion of time would serve for doing all that is either necessary, profitable, or pleasant to mankind, especially while pleasure is kept within its due bounds.

'This appears very plainly in Utopia; for there, in a great city, and in all the territory that lies round it, you can scarce find five hundred, either men or women, by their age and strength capable of labour, that are not engaged in it. Even the Syphogrants, though excused by the law, yet do not excuse themselves, but work, that by their examples they may excite the industry of the rest of the people; the like exemption is allowed to those who, being recommended to the people by the priests, are, by the secret suffrages of the Syphogrants, privileged from labour, that they may apply themselves wholly to study; and if any of these fall short of those hopes that they seemed at first to give, they are obliged to return to work; and sometimes a mechanic that so employs his leisure hours as to make a considerable advancement in learning is eased from being a tradesman and ranked among their learned men. Out of these they choose their ambassadors, their priests, their Tranibors, and the Prince himself, anciently called their Barzenes, but is called of late their Ademus.

'And thus from the great numbers among them that are neither suffered to be idle nor to be employed in any fruitless labour, you may easily make the estimate how much may be done in those few hours in which they are obliged to labour. But, besides all that has been already said, it is to be considered that the needful arts among them are managed with less labour than anywhere else. The building or the repairing of houses among us employ many hands, because often a thriftless heir suffers a house that his father built to fall into decay, so that his successor must, at a great cost, repair that which he might have kept up with a small charge; it frequently happens that the same house which one person built at a vast expense is neglected by another, who thinks he has a more delicate sense of the beauties of architecture, and he, suffering it to fall to ruin, builds another at no less charge. But among the Utopians all things are so regulated that men very seldom build upon a new piece of ground, and are not only very quick in repairing their houses, but show their foresight in preventing their decay, so that their buildings are preserved very long with but very little labour, and thus the builders, to whom that care belongs, are often without employment, except the hewing of timber and the squaring of stones, that the materials may be in readiness for raising a building very suddenly when there is any occasion for it.

'As to their clothes, observe how little work is spent in them; while they are at labour they are clothed with leather and skins, cut carelessly about them, which will last seven years, and when they appear in public they put on an upper garment which hides the other; and these are all of one colour, and that is the natural colour of the wool. As they need less woollen cloth than is used anywhere else, so that which they make use of is much less costly; they use linen cloth more, but that is prepared with less labour, and they value cloth only by the whiteness of the linen or the cleanness of the wool, without much regard to the fineness of the thread. While in other places four or five upper garments of woollen cloth of different colours, and as many vests of silk, will scarce serve one man, and while those that are nicer think ten too few, every man there is content with one, which very often serves him two years; nor is there anything that can tempt a man to desire more, for if he had them he would neither be the, warmer nor would he make one jot the better appearance for it.

'And thus, since they are all employed in some useful labour, and since they content themselves with fewer things, it falls out that there is a great abundance of all things among them; so that it frequently happens that, for want of other work, vast numbers are sent out to mend the highways; but when no public undertaking is to be performed, the hours of working are lessened. The magistrates never engage the people in unnecessary labour, since the chief end of the constitution is to regulate labour by the necessities of the public, and to allow the people as much time as is necessary for the improvement of their minds, in which they think the happiness of life consists.

Of Their Traffic

'But it is now time to explain to you the mutual intercourse of this people, their commerce, and the rules by which all things are distributed among them.

'As their cities are composed of families, so their families are made up of those that are nearly related to one another. Their women, when they grow up, are married out, but all the males, both children and grand-children, live still in the same house, in great obedience to their common parent, unless age has weakened his understanding, and in that case he that is next to him in age comes in his room; but lest any city should become either too great, or by any accident be dispeopled, provision is made that none of their cities may contain above six thousand families, besides those of the country around it. No family may have less than ten and more than sixteen persons in it, but there can be no determined number for the children under age; this rule is easily observed by removing some of the children of a more fruitful couple to any other family that does not abound so much in them.

'By the same rule they supply cities that do not increase so fast from others that breed faster; and if there is any increase over the whole island, then they draw out a number of their citizens out of the several towns and send them over to the neighbouring continent, where, if they find that the inhabitants have more soil than they can well cultivate, they fix a colony, taking the inhabitants into their society if they are willing to live with them; and where they do that of their own accord, they quickly enter into their method of life and conform to their rules, and this proves a happiness to both nations; for, according to their constitution, such care is taken of the soil that it becomes fruitful enough for both, though it might be otherwise too narrow and barren for any one of them.

'But if the natives refuse to conform themselves to their laws they drive them out of those bounds which they mark out for themselves, and use force if they resist, for they account it a very just cause of war for a nation to hinder others from possessing a part of that soil of which they make no use, but which is suffered to lie idle and uncultivated, since every man has, by the law of nature, a right to such a waste portion of the earth as is necessary for his subsistence. If an accident has so lessened the number of the inhabitants of any of their towns that it cannot be made up from the other towns of the island without diminishing them too much (which is said to have fallen out but twice since they were first a people, when great numbers were carried off by the plague), the loss is then supplied by recalling as many as are wanted from their colonies, for they will abandon these rather than suffer the towns in the island to sink too low.

'But to return to their manner of living in society: the oldest man of every family, as has been already said, is its governor; wives serve their husbands, and children their parents, and always the younger serves the elder.

'Every city is divided into four equal parts, and in the middle of each there is a market-place. What is brought thither, and manufactured by the several families, is carried from thence to houses appointed for that purpose, in which all things of a sort are laid by themselves; and thither every father goes, and takes whatsoever he or his family stand in need of, without either paying for it or leaving anything in exchange. There is no reason for giving a denial to any person, since there is such plenty of everything among them; and there is no danger of a man's asking for more than he needs; they have no inducements to do this, since they are sure they shall always be supplied: it is the fear of want that makes any of the whole race of animals either greedy or ravenous; but, besides fear, there is in man a pride that makes him fancy it a particular glory to excel others in pomp and excess; but by the laws of the Utopians, there is no room for this.

'Near these markets there are others for all sorts of provisions, where there are not only herbs, fruits, and bread, but also fish, fowl, and cattle. There are also, outside their towns, places appointed near some running water for killing their beasts and for washing away their filth, which is done by their slaves; for they suffer none of their citizens to kill their cattle, because they think that pity and good-nature, which are among the best of those affections that are born with us, are much impaired by the butchering of animals; nor do they suffer anything that is foul or unclean to be brought within their towns, lest the air should be infected by ill-smells, which might prejudice their health.

'In every street there are great halls, that lie at an equal distance from each other, distinguished by particular names. The Syphogrants dwell in those that are set over thirty families, fifteen lying on one side of it, and as many on the other. In these halls they all meet and have their repasts; the stewards of every one of them come to the market-place at an appointed hour, and according to the number of those that belong to the hall they carry home provisions.

'But they take more care of their sick than of any others; these are lodged and provided for in public hospitals. They have belonging to every town four hospitals, that are built without their walls, and are so large that they may pass for little towns; by this means, if they had ever such a number of sick persons, they could lodge them conveniently, and at such a distance that such of them as are sick of infectious diseases may be kept so far from the rest that there can be no danger of contagion. The hospitals are furnished and stored with all things that are convenient for the ease and recovery of the sick; and those that are put in them are looked after with such tender and watchful care, and are so constantly attended by their skilful physicians, that as none is sent to them against their will, so there is scarce one in a whole town that, if he should fall ill, would not choose rather to go thither than lie sick at home.

'After the steward of the hospitals has taken for the sick whatsoever the physician prescribes, then the best things that are left in the market are distributed equally among the halls in proportion to their numbers; only, in the first place, they serve the Prince, the Chief Priest, the Tranibors, the Ambassadors, and strangers, if there are any, which, indeed, falls out but seldom, and for whom there are houses, well furnished, particularly appointed for their reception when they come among them. At the hours of dinner and supper the whole Syphogranty being called together by sound of trumpet, they meet and eat together, except only such as are in the hospitals or lie sick at home. Yet, after the halls are served, no man is hindered to carry provisions home from the market-place, for they know that none does that but for some good reason; for though any that will may eat at home, yet none does it willingly, since it is both ridiculous and foolish for any to give themselves the trouble to make ready an ill dinner at home when there is a much more plentiful one made ready for him so near hand. All the uneasy and sordid services about these halls are performed by their slaves; but the dressing and cooking their meat, and the ordering their tables, belong only to the women, all those of every family taking it by turns.

'They sit at three or more tables, according to their number; the men sit towards the wall, and the women sit on the other side, that if any of them should be taken suddenly ill, which is no uncommon case amongst women with child, she may, without disturbing the rest, rise and go to the nurses' room (who are there with the suckling children), where there is always clean water at hand and cradles, in which they may lay the young children if there is occasion for it, and a fire, that they may shift and dress them before it. Every child is nursed by its own mother if death or sickness does not intervene; and in that case the Syphogrants' wives find out a nurse quickly, which is no hard matter, for any one that can do it offers herself cheerfully; for as they are much inclined to that piece of mercy, so the child whom they nurse considers the nurse as its mother. All the children under five years old sit among the nurses; the rest of the younger sort of both sexes, till they are fit for marriage, either serve those that sit at table, or, if they are not strong enough for that, stand by them in great silence and eat what is given them; nor have they any other formality of dining.

'In the middle of the first table, which stands across the upper end of the hall, sit the Syphogrant and his wife, for that is the chief and most conspicuous place; next to him sit two of the most ancient, for there go always four to a mess. If there is a temple within the Syphogranty, the Priest and his wife sit with the Syphogrant above all the rest; next them there is a mixture of old and young, who are so placed that as the young are set near others, so they are mixed with the more ancient; which, they say, was appointed on this account: that the gravity of the old people, and the reverence that is due to them, might restrain the younger from all indecent words and gestures. Dishes are not served up to the whole table at first, but the best are first set before the old, whose seats are distinguished from the young, and, after them, all the rest are served alike. The old men distribute to the younger any curious meats that happen to be set before them, if there is not such an abundance of them that the whole company may be served alike.

'Thus old men are honoured with a particular respect, yet all the rest fare as well as they.

'Both dinner and supper are begun with some lecture of morality that is read to them; but it is so short that it is not tedious nor uneasy to them to hear it. From hence the old men take occasion to entertain those about them with some useful and pleasant enlargements; but they do not engross the whole discourse so to themselves during their meals that the younger may not put in for a share; on the contrary, they engage them to talk, that so they may, in that free way of conversation, find out the force of every one's spirit and observe his temper.

'They despatch their dinners quickly, but sit long at supper, because they go to work after the one, and are to sleep after the other, during which they think the stomach carries on the concoction more vigorously. They never sup without music, and there is always fruit served up after meat; while they are at table some burn perfumes and sprinkle about fragrant ointments and sweet waters – in short, they want nothing that may cheer up their spirits; they give themselves a large allowance that way, and indulge themselves in all such pleasures as are attended with no inconvenience. Thus do those that are in the towns live together; but in the country, where they live at a great distance, every one eats at home, and no family wants any necessary sort of provision, for it is from them that provisions are sent unto those that live in the towns.

Of the Travelling of the Utopians

'If any man has a mind to visit his friends that live in some other town, or desires to travel and see the rest of the country, he obtains leave very easily from the Syphogrant and Tranibors, when there is no particular occasion for him at home. Such as travel carry with them a passport from the Prince, which both certifies the licence that is granted for travelling, and limits the time of their return. They are furnished with a wagon and a slave, who drives the oxen and looks after them; but, unless there are women in the company, the wagon is sent back at the end of the journey as a needless encumbrance. While they are on the road they carry no provisions with them, yet they want for nothing, but are everywhere treated as if they were at home. If they stay in any place longer than a night, every one follows his proper occupation, and is very well used by those of his own trade; but if any man goes out of the city to which he belongs without leave, and is found rambling without a passport, he is severely treated, he is punished as a fugitive, and sent home disgracefully; and, if he falls again into the like fault, is condemned to slavery. If any man has a mind to travel only over the precinct of his own city, he may freely do it, with his father's permission and his wife's consent; but when he comes into any of the country houses, if he expects to be entertained by them, he must labour with them and conform to their rules; and if he does this, he may freely go over the whole precinct, being then as useful to the city to which he belongs as if he were still within it.

'Thus you see that there are no idle persons among them, nor pretences of excusing any from labour. There are no taverns, no ale-houses, nor stews among them, nor any other occasions of corrupting each other, of getting into corners, or forming themselves into parties; all men live in full view, so that all are obliged both to perform their ordinary task and to employ themselves well in their spare hours; and it is certain that a people thus ordered must live in great abundance of all things, and these being equally distributed among them, no man can want or be obliged to beg.

'In their great council at Amaurot, to which there are three sent from every town once a year, they examine what towns abound in provisions and what are under any scarcity, that so the one may be furnished from the other; and this is done freely, without any sort of exchange; for, according to their plenty or scarcity, they supply or are supplied from one another, so that indeed the whole island is, as it were, one family.

'When they have thus taken care of their whole country, and laid up stores for two years (which they do to prevent the ill consequences of an unfavourable season), they order an exportation of the surplus, both of corn, honey, wool, flax, wood, wax, tallow, leather, and cattle, which they send out, commonly in great quantities, to other nations. They order a seventh part of all these goods to be freely given to the poor of the countries to which they send them, and sell the rest at moderate rates; and by this exchange they not only bring back those few things that they need at home (for, indeed, they scarce need anything but iron), but likewise a great deal of gold and silver; and by their driving this trade so long, it is not to be imagined how vast a treasure they have got among them, so that now they do not much care whether they sell off their merchandise for money in hand or upon trust.

'A great part of their treasure is now in bonds; but in all their contracts no private man stands bound, but the writing runs in the name of the town; and the towns that owe them money raise it from those private hands that owe it to them, lay it up in their public chamber, or enjoy the profit of it till the Utopians call for it; and they choose rather to let the greatest part of it lie in their hands, who make advantage by it, than to call for it themselves; but if they see that any of their other neighbours stand more in need of it, then they call it in and lend it to them.

'Whenever they are engaged in war, which is the only occasion in which their treasure can be usefully employed, they make use of it themselves; in great extremities or sudden accidents they employ it in hiring foreign troops, whom they more willingly expose to danger than their own people; they give them great pay, knowing well that this will work even on their enemies; that it will engage them either to betray their own side, or, at least, to desert it; and that it is the best means of raising mutual jealousies among them.

'For this end they have an incredible treasure; but they do not keep it as a treasure, but in such a manner as I am almost afraid to tell, lest you think it so extravagant as to be hardly credible. This I have the more reason to apprehend because, if I had not seen it myself, I could not have been easily persuaded to have believed it upon any man's report.

'It is certain that all things appear incredible to us in proportion as they differ from known customs; but one who can judge aright will not wonder to find that, since their constitution differs so much from ours, their value of gold and silver should be measured by a very different standard; for since they have no use for money among themselves, but keep it as a provision against events which seldom happen, and between which there are generally long intervening intervals, they value it no farther than it deserves – that is, in proportion to its use. So that it is plain they must prefer iron either to gold or silver, for men can no more live without iron than without fire or water; but Nature has marked out no use for the other metals so essential as not easily to be dispensed with. The folly of men has enhanced the value of gold and silver because of their scarcity; whereas, on the contrary, it is their opinion that Nature, as an indulgent parent, has freely given us all the best things in great abundance, such as water and earth, but has laid up and hid from us the things that are vain and useless.

'If these metals were laid up in any tower in the kingdom it would raise a jealousy of the Prince and Senate, and give birth to that foolish mistrust into which the people are apt to fall – a jealousy of their intending to sacrifice the interest of the public to their own private advantage. If they should work it into vessels, or any sort of plate, they fear that the people might grow too fond of it, and so be unwilling to let the plate be run down, if a war made it necessary, to employ it in paying their soldiers. To prevent all these inconveniences they have fallen upon an expedient which, as it agrees with their other policy, so is it very different from ours, and will scarce gain belief among us who value gold so much, and lay it up so carefully. They eat and drink out of vessels of earth or glass, which make an agreeable appearance, though formed of brittle materials; while they make their chamber-pots and close-stools of gold and silver, and that not only in their public halls but in their private houses. Of the same metals they likewise make chains and fetters for their slaves, to some of which, as a badge of infamy, they hang an earring of gold, and make others wear a chain or a coronet of the same metal; and thus they take care by all possible means to render gold and silver of no esteem; and from hence it is that while other nations part with their gold and silver as unwillingly as if one tore out their bowels, those of Utopia would look on their giving in all they possess of those metals (when there were any use for them) but as the parting with a trifle, or as we would esteem the loss of a penny!

'They find pearls on their coasts, and diamonds and carbuncles on their rocks; they do not look after them, but, if they find them by chance, they polish them, and with them they adorn their children, who are delighted with them, and glory in them during their childhood; but when they grow to years, and see that none but children use such baubles, they of their own accord, without being bid by their parents, lay them aside, and would be as much ashamed to use them afterwards as children among us, when they come to years, are of their puppets and other toys.

'I never saw a clearer instance of the opposite impressions that different customs make on people than I observed in the ambassadors of the Anemolians, who came to Amaurot when I was there. As they came to treat of affairs of great consequence, the deputies from several towns met together to wait for their coming. The ambassadors of the nations that lie near Utopia, knowing their customs, and that fine clothes are in no esteem among them, that silk is despised, and gold is a badge of infamy, used to come very modestly clothed; but the Anemolians, lying more remote, and having had little commerce with them, understanding that they were coarsely clothed, and all in the same manner, took it for granted that they had none of those fine things among them of which they made no use; and they, being a vainglorious rather than a wise people, resolved to set themselves out with so much pomp that they should look like gods, and strike the eyes of the poor Utopians with their splendour.

'Thus three ambassadors made their entry with a hundred attendants, all clad in garments of different colours, and the greater part in silk; the ambassadors themselves, who were of the nobility of their country, were in cloth-of-gold, and adorned with massy chains, earrings and rings of gold; their caps were covered with bracelets set full of pearls and other gems – in a word, they were set out with all those things that among the Utopians were either the badges of slavery, the marks of infamy, or the playthings of children. It was not unpleasant to see, on the one side, how they looked big, when they compared their rich habits with the plain clothes of the Utopians, who were come out in great numbers to see them make their entry; and, on the other, to observe how much they were mistaken in the impression which they hoped this pomp would have made on them. It appeared so ridiculous a show to all that had never stirred out of their country, and had not seen the customs of other nations, that though they paid some reverence to those that were the most meanly clad, as if they had been the ambassadors, yet when they saw the ambassadors themselves so full of gold and chains, they looked upon them as slaves, and forbore to treat them with reverence.

'You might have seen the children who were grown big enough to despise their playthings, and who had thrown away their jewels, call to their mothers, push them gently, and cry out, "See that great fool, that wears pearls and gems as if he were yet a child!" While their mothers very innocently replied, "Hold your peace! This, I believe, is one of the ambassadors' fools." Others censured the fashion of their chains, and observed, "That they were of no use, for they were too slight to bind their slaves, who could easily break them; and, besides, hung so loose about them that they thought it easy to throw theirs away, and so get from them."

'But after the ambassadors had stayed a day among them, and saw so vast a quantity of gold in their houses (which was as much despised by them as it was esteemed in other nations), and beheld more gold and silver in the chains and fetters of one slave than all their ornaments amounted to, their plumes fell, and they were ashamed of all that glory for which they had formed valued themselves, and accordingly laid it aside – a resolution that they immediately took when, on their engaging in some free discourse with the Utopians, they discovered their sense of such things and their other customs.

'The Utopians wonder how any man should be so much taken with the glaring doubtful lustre of a jewel or a stone, that can look up to a star or to the sun himself; or how any should value himself because his cloth is made of a finer thread; for, how fine soever that thread may be, it was once no better than the fleece of a sheep, and that sheep, was a sheep still, for all its wearing it. They wonder much to hear that gold, which in itself is so useless a thing, should be everywhere so much esteemed that even man, for whom it was made, and by whom it has its value, should yet be thought of less value than this metal; that a blockhead, who has no more sense than a log of wood, and is as bad as he is foolish, should have many wise and good men to serve him, only because he has a great heap of that metal; and that if it should happen that by some accident or trick of law (which, sometimes produces as great changes as chance itself) all this wealth should pass from the master to the meanest varlet of his whole family, he himself would very soon become one of his servants, as if he were a thing that belonged to his wealth, and so were bound to follow its fortune! But they much more wonder at and detest the folly of those who, when they see a rich man, though they neither owe him anything, nor are in any sort dependent on his bounty, yet, merely because he is rich, give him little less than divine honours, even though they know him to be so covetous and base-minded that, notwithstanding all his wealth, he will not part with one farthing of it to them as long as he lives!

'These and such like notions have that people imbibed, partly from their education, being bred in a country whose customs and laws are opposite to all such foolish maxims, and partly from their learning and studies – for though there are but few in any town that are so wholly excused from labour as to give themselves entirely up to their studies (these being only such persons as discover from their childhood an extraordinary capacity and disposition for letters), yet their children and a great part of the nation, both men and women, are taught to spend those hours in which they are not obliged to work in reading; and this they do through the whole progress of life.

'They have all their learning in their own tongue, which is both a copious and pleasant language, and in which a man can fully express his mind; it runs over a great tract of many countries, but it is not equally pure in all places.

'They had never so much as heard of the names of any of those philosophers that are so famous in these parts of the world, before we went among them; and yet they had made the same discoveries as the Greeks, both in music, logic, arithmetic, and geometry. But as they are almost in everything equal to the ancient philosophers, so they far exceed our modern logicians for they have never yet fallen upon the barbarous niceties that our youth are forced to learn in those trifling logical schools that are among us. They are so far from minding chimeras and fantastical images made in the mind that none of them could comprehend what we meant when we talked to them of a man in the abstract as common to all men in particular (so that though we spoke of him as a thing that we could point at with our fingers, yet none of them could perceive him) and yet distinct from every one, as if he were some monstrous Colossus or giant; yet, for all this ignorance of these empty notions, they knew astronomy, and were perfectly acquainted with the motions of the heavenly bodies; and have many instruments, well contrived and divided, by which they very accurately compute the course and positions of the sun, moon, and stars. But for the cheat of divining by the stars, by their oppositions or conjunctions, it has not so much as entered into their thoughts. They have a particular sagacity, founded upon much observation, in judging of the weather, by which they know when they may look for rain, wind, or other alterations in the air; but as to the philosophy of these things, the cause of the saltness of the sea, of its ebbing and flowing, and of the original and nature both of the heavens and the earth, they dispute of them partly as our ancient philosophers have done, and partly upon some new hypothesis, in which, as they differ from them, so they do not in all things agree among themselves.

'As to moral philosophy, they have the same disputes among them as we have here. They examine what are properly good, both for the body and the mind; and whether any outward thing can be called truly *good*, or if that term belong only to the endowments of the soul. They inquire, likewise, into the nature of virtue and pleasure. But their chief dispute is concerning the happiness of a man, and wherein it consists – whether in some one thing or in a great many. They seem, indeed, more inclinable to that opinion that places, if not the whole, yet the chief part, of a man's happiness in pleasure; and, what may seem more strange, they make use of arguments even from religion, notwithstanding its severity and roughness, for the support of that opinion so indulgent to pleasure; for they never dispute concerning happiness without fetching some arguments from the principles of religion as well as from natural reason, since without the former they reckon that all our inquiries after happiness must be but conjectural and defective.

'These are their religious principles: That the soul of man is immortal, and that God of His goodness has designed that it should be happy; and that He has, therefore, appointed rewards for good and virtuous actions, and punishments for vice, to be distributed after this life. Though these principles of religion are conveyed down among them by tradition, they think that even reason itself determines a man to believe and acknowledge them; and freely confess that if these were taken away, no man would be so insensible as not to seek after pleasure by all possible means, lawful or unlawful, using only this caution – that a lesser pleasure might not stand in the way of a greater, and that no pleasure ought to be pursued that should draw a great deal of pain after it; for they think it the maddest thing in the world to pursue virtue, that is a sour and difficult thing, and not only to renounce the pleasures of life, but willingly to undergo much pain and trouble, if a man has no prospect of a reward. And what reward can there be for one that has passed his whole life, not only without pleasure, but in pain, if there is nothing to be expected after death? Yet they do not place happiness in all sorts of pleasures, but only in those that in themselves are good and honest.

'There is a party among them who place happiness in bare virtue; others think that our natures are conducted by virtue to happiness, as that which is the chief good of man. They define virtue thus – that it is a living according to Nature, and think that we are made by God for that end; they believe that a man then follows the dictates of Nature when he pursues or avoids things according to the direction of reason. They say that the first dictate of reason is the kindling in us a love and reverence for the Divine Majesty, to whom we owe both all that we have and, all that we can ever hope for. In the next place, reason directs us to keep our minds as free from passion and as cheerful as we can, and that we should consider ourselves as bound by the ties of good nature and humanity to use our utmost endeavours to help forward the happiness of all other persons; for there never was any man such a morose and severe pursuer of virtue, such an enemy to pleasure, that though he set hard rules for men to undergo, much pain, many watchings, and other rigors, yet did not at the same time advise them to do all they could in order to relieve and ease the miserable, and who did not represent gentleness and good-nature as amiable dispositions. And from thence they infer that if a man ought to advance the welfare and comfort of the rest of mankind (there being no virtue more proper and peculiar to our nature than to ease the miseries of others, to free from trouble and anxiety, in furnishing them with the comforts of life, in which pleasure consists) Nature much more vigorously leads them to do all this for himself. A life of pleasure is either a real evil, and in that case we ought not to assist others in their pursuit of it, but, on the contrary, to keep them from it all we can, as from that which is most hurtful and deadly; or if it is a good thing, so that we not only may but ought to help others to it, why, then, ought not a man to begin with himself? – since no man can be more bound to look after the good of another than after his own; for Nature cannot direct us to be good and kind to others, and yet at the same time to be unmerciful and cruel to ourselves. Thus as they define virtue to be living according to Nature, so they imagine that Nature prompts all people on to seek after pleasure as the end of all they do.

'They also observe that in order to our supporting the pleasures of life, Nature inclines us to enter into society; for there is no man so much raised above the rest of mankind as to be the only favourite of Nature, who, on the contrary, seems to have placed on a level all those that belong to the same species. Upon this they infer that no man ought to seek his own conveniences so eagerly as to prejudice others; and therefore they think that not only all agreements between private persons ought to be observed, but likewise that all those laws ought to be kept which either a good prince has published in due form, or to which a people that is neither oppressed with tyranny nor circumvented by fraud has consented, for distributing those conveniences of life which afford us all our pleasures.

'They think it is an evidence of true wisdom for a man to pursue his own advantage as far as the laws allow it, they account it piety to prefer the public good to one's private concerns, but they think it unjust for a man to seek for pleasure by snatching another man's pleasures from him; and, on the contrary, they think it a sign of a gentle and good soul for a man to dispense with his own advantage for the good of others, and that by this means a good man finds as much pleasure one way as he parts with another; for as he may expect the like from others when he may come to need it, so, if that should fail him, yet the sense of a good action, and the reflections that he makes on the love and gratitude of those whom he has so obliged, gives the mind more pleasure than the body could have found in that from which it had restrained itself. They are also persuaded that God will make up the loss of those small pleasures with a vast and endless joy, of which religion easily convinces a good soul.

'Thus, upon an inquiry into the whole matter, they reckon that all our actions, and even all our virtues, terminate in pleasure, as in our chief end and greatest happiness; and they call every motion or state, either of body or mind, in which Nature teaches us to delight, a pleasure. Thus they cautiously limit pleasure only to those appetites to which Nature leads us; for they say that Nature leads us only to those delights to which reason, as well as sense, carries us, and by which we neither injure any other person nor lose the possession of greater pleasures, and of such as draw no troubles after them. But they look upon those delights which men by a foolish, though common, mistake call pleasure, as if they could change as easily the nature of things as the use of words, as things that greatly obstruct their real happiness, instead of advancing it, because they so entirely possess the minds of those that are once captivated by them with a false notion of pleasure that there is no room left for pleasures of a truer or purer kind.

'There are many things that in themselves have nothing that is truly delightful; on the contrary, they have a good deal of bitterness in them; and yet, from our perverse appetites after forbidden objects, are not only ranked among the pleasures, but are made even the greatest designs, of life. Among those who pursue these sophisticated pleasures they reckon such as I mentioned before, who think themselves really the better for having fine clothes; in which they think they are doubly mistaken, both in the opinion they have of their clothes, and in that they have of themselves. For if you consider the use of clothes, why should a fine thread be thought better than a coarse one? And yet these men, as if they had some real advantages beyond others, and did not owe them wholly to their mistakes, look big, seem to fancy themselves to be more valuable, and imagine that a respect is due to them for the sake of a rich garment, to which they would not have pretended if they had been more meanly clothed, and even resent it as an affront if that respect is not paid them.

'It is also a great folly to be taken with outward marks of respect, which signify nothing; for what true or real pleasure can one man find in another's standing bare or making legs to him? Will the bending another man's knees give ease to yours? And will the head's being bare cure the madness of yours? And yet it is wonderful to see how this false notion of pleasure bewitches many who delight themselves with the fancy of their nobility, and are pleased with this conceit – that they are descended from ancestors who have been held for some successions rich, and who have had great possessions; for this is all that makes nobility at present. Yet they do not think themselves a whit the less noble, though their immediate parents have left none of this wealth to them, or though they themselves have squandered it away.

'The Utopians have no better opinion of those who are much taken with gems and precious stones, and who account it a degree of happiness next to a divine one if they can purchase one that is very extraordinary, especially if it be of that sort of stones that is then in greatest request, for the same sort is not at all times universally of the same value, nor will men buy it unless it be dismounted and taken out of the gold. The jeweller is then made to give good security, and required solemnly to swear that the stone is true, that, by such an exact caution, a false one might not be bought instead of a true; though, if you were to examine it, your eye could find no difference between the counterfeit and that which is true; so that they are all one to you, as much as if you were blind. Or can it be thought that they who heap up a useless mass of wealth, not for any use that it is to bring them, but merely to please themselves with the contemplation of it, enjoy any true pleasure in it? The delight they find is only a false shadow of joy. Those are no better whose error is somewhat different from the former, and who hide it out of their fear of losing it; for what other name can fit the hiding it in the earth, or, rather, the restoring it to it again, it being thus cut off from being useful either to its owner or to the rest of mankind? And yet the owner, having hid it carefully, is glad, because he thinks he is now sure of it. If it should be stole, the owner, though he might live perhaps ten years after the theft, of which he knew nothing, would find no difference between his having or losing it, for both ways it was equally useless to him.

'Among those foolish pursuers of pleasure they reckon all that delight in hunting, in fowling, or gaming, of whose madness they have only heard, for they have no such things among them. But they have asked us, "What sort of pleasure is it that men can find in throwing the dice?" (for if there were any pleasure in it, they think the doing it so often should give one a surfeit of it); "and what pleasure can one find in hearing the barking and howling of dogs, which seem rather odious than pleasant sounds?" Nor can they comprehend the pleasure of seeing dogs run after a hare, more than of seeing one dog run after another; for if the seeing them run is that which gives the pleasure, you have the same entertainment to the eye on both these occasions, since that is the same in both cases. But if the pleasure lies in seeing the hare killed and torn by the dogs, this ought rather to stir pity, that a weak, harmless, and fearful hare should be devoured by strong, fierce, and cruel dogs. Therefore all this business of hunting is, among the Utopians, turned over to their butchers, and those, as has been already said, are all slaves, and they look on hunting as one of the basest parts of a butcher's work, for they account it both more profitable and more decent to kill those beasts that are more necessary and useful to mankind, whereas the killing and tearing of so small and miserable an animal can only attract the huntsman with a false show of pleasure, from which he can reap but small advantage. They look on the desire of the bloodshed, even of beasts, as a mark of a mind that is already corrupted with cruelty, or that at least, by too frequent returns of so brutal a pleasure, must degenerate into it.

'Thus though the rabble of mankind look upon these, and on innumerable other things of the same nature, as pleasures, the Utopians, on the contrary, observing that there is nothing in them truly pleasant, conclude that they are not to be reckoned among pleasures; for though these things may create some tickling in the senses (which seems to be a true notion of pleasure), yet they imagine that this does not arise from the thing itself, but from a depraved custom, which may so vitiate a man's taste that bitter things may pass for sweet, as women with child think pitch or tallow taste sweeter than honey; but as a man's sense, when corrupted either by a disease or some ill habit, does not change the nature of other things, so neither can it change the nature of pleasure.

'They reckon up several sorts of pleasures, which they call true ones; some belong to the body, and others to the mind. The pleasures of the mind lie in knowledge, and in that delight which the contemplation of truth carries with it; to which they add the joyful reflections on a well-spent life, and the assured hopes of a future happiness. They divide the pleasures of the body into two sorts – the one is that which gives our senses some real delight, and is performed either by recruiting Nature and supplying those parts which feed the internal heat of life by eating and drinking, or when Nature is eased of any surcharge that oppresses it, when we are relieved from sudden pain, or that which arises from satisfying the appetite which Nature has wisely given to lead us to the propagation of the species. There is another kind of pleasure that arises neither from our receiving what the body requires, nor its being relieved when overcharged, and yet, by a secret unseen virtue, affects the senses, raises the passions, and strikes the mind with generous impressions — this is, the pleasure that arises from music. Another kind of bodily pleasure is that which results from an undisturbed and vigorous constitution of body, when life and active spirits seem to actuate every part. This lively health, when entirely free from all mixture of pain, of itself gives an inward pleasure, independent of all external objects of delight; and though this pleasure does not so powerfully affect us, nor act so strongly on the senses as some of the others, yet it may be esteemed as the greatest of all pleasures; and almost all the Utopians reckon it the foundation and basis of all the other joys of life, since this alone makes the state of life easy and desirable, and when this is wanting, a man is really capable of no other pleasure. They look upon freedom from pain, if it does not rise from perfect health, to be a state of stupidity rather than of pleasure. This subject has been very narrowly canvassed among them, and it has been debated whether a firm and entire health could be called a pleasure or not.

'Some have thought that there was no pleasure but what was "excited" by some sensible motion in the body. But this opinion has been long ago excluded from among them; so that now they almost universally agree that health is the greatest of all bodily pleasures; and that as there is a pain in sickness which is as opposite in its nature to pleasure as sickness itself is to health, so they hold that health is accompanied with pleasure. And if any should say that sickness is not really pain, but that it only carries pain along with it, they look upon that as a fetch of subtlety that does not much alter the matter. It is all one, in their opinion, whether it be said that health is in itself a pleasure, or that it begets a pleasure, as fire gives heat, so it be granted that all those whose health is entire have a true pleasure in the enjoyment of it. And they reason thus: "What is the pleasure of eating, but that a man's health, which had been weakened, does, with the assistance of food, drive away hunger, and so recruiting itself, recovers its former vigour? And being thus refreshed it finds a pleasure in that conflict; and if the conflict is pleasure, the victory must yet breed a greater pleasure, except we fancy that it becomes stupid as soon as it has obtained that which it pursued, and so neither knows nor rejoices in its own welfare." If it is said that health cannot be felt, they absolutely deny it; for what man is in health, that does not perceive it when he is awake? Is there any man that is so dull and stupid as not to acknowledge that he feels a delight in health? And what is delight but another name for pleasure?

'But, of all pleasures, they esteem those to be most valuable that lie in the mind, the chief of which arise out of true virtue and the witness of a good conscience. They account health the chief pleasure that belongs to the body; for they think that the pleasure of eating and drinking, and all the other delights of sense, are only so far desirable as they give or maintain health; but they are not pleasant in themselves otherwise than as they resist those impressions that our natural infirmities are still making upon us. For as a wise man desires rather to avoid diseases than to take physic, and to be freed from pain rather than to find ease by remedies, so it is more desirable not to need this sort of pleasure than to be obliged to indulge it.

'If any man imagines that there is a real happiness in these enjoyments, he must then confess that he would be the happiest of all men if he were to lead his life in perpetual hunger, thirst, and itching, and, by consequence, in perpetual eating, drinking, and scratching himself; which any one may easily see would be not only a base, but a miserable, state of a life. These are, indeed, the lowest of pleasures, and the least pure, for we can never relish them but when they are mixed with the contrary pains. The pain of hunger must give us the pleasure of eating, and here the pain out-balances the pleasure. And as the pain is more vehement, so it lasts much longer; for as it begins before the pleasure, so it does not cease but with the pleasure that extinguishes it, and both expire together. They think, therefore, none of those pleasures are to be valued any further than as they are necessary; yet they rejoice in them, and with due gratitude acknowledge the tenderness of the great Author of Nature, who has planted in us appetites, by which those things that are necessary for our preservation are likewise made pleasant to us. For how miserable a thing would life be if those daily diseases of hunger and thirst were to be carried off by such bitter drugs as we must use for those diseases that return seldomer upon us! And thus these pleasant, as well as proper, gifts of Nature maintain the strength and the sprightliness of our bodies.

'They also entertain themselves with the other delights let in at their eyes, their ears, and their nostrils as the pleasant relishes and seasoning of life, which Nature seems to have marked out peculiarly for man, since no other sort of animals contemplates the figure and beauty of the universe, nor is delighted with smells any further than as they distinguish meats by them; nor do they apprehend the concords or discords of sound. Yet, in all pleasures whatsoever, they take care that a lesser joy does not hinder a greater, and that pleasure may never breed pain, which they think always follows dishonest pleasures. But they think it madness for a man to wear out the beauty of his face or the force of his natural strength, to corrupt the sprightliness of his body by sloth and laziness, or to waste it by fasting; that it is madness to weaken the strength of his constitution and reject the other delights of life, unless by renouncing his own satisfaction he can either serve the public or promote the happiness of others, for which he expects a greater recompense from God. So that they look on such a course of life as the mark of a mind that is both cruel to itself and ungrateful to the Author of Nature, as if we would not be beholden to Him for His favours, and therefore rejects all His blessings; as one who should afflict himself for the empty shadow of virtue, or for no better end than to render himself capable of bearing those misfortunes which possibly will never happen.

'This is their notion of virtue and of pleasure: they think that no man's reason can carry him to a truer idea of them unless some discovery from heaven should inspire him with sublimer notions. I have not now the leisure to examine whether they think right or wrong in this matter; nor do I judge it necessary, for I have only undertaken to give you an account of their constitution, but not to defend all their principles. I am sure that whatever may be said of their notions, there is not in the whole world either a better people or a happier government. Their bodies are vigorous and lively; and though they are but of a middle stature, and have neither the fruitfullest soil nor the purest air in the world; yet they fortify themselves so well, by their temperate course of life, against the unhealthiness of their air, and by their industry they so cultivate their soil, that there is nowhere to be seen a greater increase, both of corn and cattle, nor are there anywhere healthier men and freer from diseases; for one may there see reduced to practice not only all the art that the husbandman employs in manuring and improving an ill soil, but whole woods plucked up by the roots, and in other places new ones planted, where there were none before. Their principal motive for this is the convenience of carriage, that their timber may be either near their towns or growing on the banks of the sea, or of some rivers, so as to be floated to them; for it is a harder work to carry wood at any distance over land than corn. The people are industrious, apt to learn, as well as cheerful and pleasant, and none can endure more labour when it is necessary; but, except in that case, they love their ease.

'They are unwearied pursuers of knowledge; for when we had given them some hints of the learning and discipline of the Greeks, concerning whom we only instructed them (for we know that there was nothing among the Romans, except their historians and their poets, that they would value much), it was strange to see how eagerly they were set on learning that language: we began to read a little of it to them, rather in compliance with their importunity than out of any hopes of their reaping from it any great advantage: but, after a very short trial, we found they made such progress, that we saw our labour was like to be more successful than we could have expected: they learned to write their characters and to pronounce their language so exactly, had so quick an apprehension, they remembered it so faithfully, and became so ready and correct in the use of it, that it would have looked like a miracle if the greater part of those whom we taught had not been men both of extraordinary capacity and of a fit age for instruction: they were, for the greatest part, chosen from among their learned men by their chief council, though some studied it of their own accord. In three years' time they became masters of the whole language, so that they read the best of the Greek authors very exactly. I am, indeed, apt to think that they learned that language the more easily from its having some relation to their own. I believe that they were a colony of the Greeks; for though their language comes nearer the Persian, yet they retain many names, both for their towns and magistrates, that are of Greek derivation.

'I happened to carry a great many books with me, instead of merchandise, when I sailed my fourth voyage; for I was so far from thinking of soon coming back, that I rather thought never to have returned at all, and I gave them all my books, among which were many of Plato's and some of Aristotle's works: I had also Theophrastus on Plants, which, to my great regret, was imperfect; for having laid it carelessly by, while we were at sea, a monkey had seized upon it, and in many places torn out the leaves. They have no books of grammar but Lascares, for I did not carry Theodorus with me; nor have they any dictionaries but Hesichius and Dioscerides. They esteem Plutarch highly, and were much taken with Lucian's wit and with his pleasant way of writing. As for the poets, they have Aristophanes, Homer, Euripides, and Sophocles of Aldus's edition; and for historians, Thucydides, Herodotus, and Herodian.

'One of my companions, Thricius Apinatus, happened to carry with him some of Hippocrates' works and Galen's Microtechne, which they hold in great estimation; for though there is no nation in the world that needs physic so little as they do, yet there is not any that honours it so much; they reckon the knowledge of it one of the pleasantest and most profitable parts of philosophy, by which, as they search into the secrets of nature, so they not only find this study highly agreeable, but think that such inquiries are very acceptable to the Author of nature; and imagine, that as He, like the inventors of curious engines amongst mankind, has exposed this great machine of the universe to the view of the only creatures capable of contemplating it, so an exact and curious observer, who admires His workmanship, is much more acceptable to Him than one of the herd, who, like a beast incapable of reason, looks on this glorious scene with the eyes of a dull and unconcerned spectator.

'The minds of the Utopians, when fenced with a love for learning, are very ingenious in discovering all such arts as are necessary to carry it to perfection. Two things they owe to us, the manufacture of paper and the art of printing; yet they are not so entirely indebted to us for these discoveries but that a great part of the invention was their own. We showed them some books printed by Aldus, we explained to them the way of making paper and the mystery of printing; but, as we had never practised these arts, we described them in a crude and superficial manner. They seized the hints we gave them; and though at first they could not arrive at perfection, yet by making many essays they at last found out and corrected all their errors and conquered every difficulty. Before this they only wrote on parchment, on reeds, or on the barks of trees; but now they have established the manufactures of paper and set up printing presses, so that, if they had but a good number of Greek authors, they would be quickly supplied with many copies of them: at present, though they have no more than those I have mentioned, yet, by several impressions, they have multiplied them into many thousands.

'If any man was to go among them that had some extraordinary talent, or that by much travelling had observed the customs of many nations (which made us to be so well received), he would receive a hearty welcome, for they are very desirous to know the state of the whole world. Very few go among them on the account of traffic; for what can a man carry to them but iron, or gold, or silver? – which merchants desire rather to export than import to a strange country: and as for their exportation, they think it better to manage that themselves than to leave it to foreigners, for by this means, as they understand the state of the neighbouring countries better, so they keep up the art of navigation which cannot be maintained but by much practice.

Of Their Slaves and of Their Marriages

'They do not make slaves of prisoners of war, except those that are taken in battle, nor of the sons of their slaves, nor of those of other nations: the slaves among them are only such as are condemned to that state of life for the commission of some crime, or, which is more common, such as their merchants find condemned to die in those parts to which they trade, whom they sometimes redeem at low rates, and in other places have them for nothing. They are kept at perpetual labour, and are always chained, but with this difference, that their own natives are treated much worse than others: they are considered as more profligate than the rest, and since they could not be restrained by the advantages of so excellent an education, are judged worthy of harder usage. Another sort of slaves are the poor of the neighbouring countries, who offer of their own accord to come and serve them: they treat these better, and use them in all other respects as well as their own countrymen, except their imposing more labour upon them, which is no hard task to those that have been accustomed to it; and if any of these have a mind to go back to their own country, which, indeed, falls out but seldom, as they do not force them to stay, so they do not send them away empty-handed.

'I have already told you with what care they look after their sick, so that nothing is left undone that can contribute either to their case or health; and for those who are taken with fixed and incurable diseases, they use all possible ways to cherish them and to make their lives as comfortable as possible. They visit them often and take great pains to make their time pass off easily; but when any is taken with a torturing and lingering pain, so that there is no hope either of recovery or ease, the priests and magistrates come and exhort them, that, since they are now unable to go on with the business of life, are become a burden to themselves and to all about them, and they have really outlived themselves, they should no longer nourish such a rooted distemper, but choose rather to die since they cannot live but in much misery; being assured that if they thus deliver themselves from torture, or are willing that others should do it, they shall be happy after death: since, by their acting thus, they lose none of the pleasures, but only the troubles of life, they think they behave not only reasonably but in a manner consistent with religion and piety; because they follow the advice given them by their priests, who are the expounders of the will of God. Such as are wrought on by these persuasions either starve themselves of their own accord, or take opium, and by that means die without pain.

'But no man is forced on this way of ending his life; and if they cannot be persuaded to it, this does not induce them to fail in their attendance and care of them: but as they believe that a voluntary death, when it is chosen upon such an authority, is very honourable, so if any man takes away his own life without the approbation of the priests and the senate, they give him none of the honours of a decent funeral, but throw his body into a ditch.

'Their women are not married before eighteen nor their men before two-and-twenty, and if any of them run into forbidden embraces before marriage they are severely punished, and the privilege of marriage is denied them unless they can obtain a special warrant from the Prince. Such disorders cast a great reproach upon the master and mistress of the family in which they happen, for it is supposed that they have failed in their duty. The reason of punishing this so severely is, because they think that if they were not strictly restrained from all vagrant appetites, very few would engage in a state in which they venture the quiet of their whole lives, by being confined to one person, and are obliged to endure all the inconveniences with which it is accompanied.

'In choosing their wives they use a method that would appear to us very absurd and ridiculous, but it is constantly observed among them, and is accounted perfectly consistent with wisdom. Before marriage some grave matron presents the bride, naked, whether she is a virgin or a widow, to the bridegroom, and after that some grave man presents the bridegroom, naked, to the bride. We, indeed, both laughed at this, and condemned it as very indecent. But they, on the other hand, wondered at the folly of the men of all other nations, who, if they are but to buy a horse of a small value, are so cautious that they will see every part of him, and take off both his saddle and all his other tackle, that there may be no secret ulcer hid under any of them, and that yet in the choice of a wife, on which depends the happiness or unhappiness of the rest of his life, a man should venture upon trust, and only see about a handsbreadth of the face, all the rest of the body being covered, under which may lie hid what may be contagious as well as loathsome. All men are not so wise as to choose a woman only for her good qualities, and even wise men consider the body as that which adds not a little to the mind, and it is certain there may be some such deformity covered with clothes as may totally alienate a man from his wife, when it is too late to part with her; if such a thing is discovered after marriage a man has no remedy but patience; they, therefore, think it is reasonable that there should be good provision made against such mischievous frauds.

'There was so much the more reason for them to make a regulation in this matter, because they are the only people of those parts that neither allow of polygamy nor of divorces, except in the case of adultery or insufferable perverseness, for in these cases the Senate dissolves the marriage and grants the injured person leave to marry again; but the guilty are made infamous and are never allowed the privilege of a second marriage. None are suffered to put away their wives against their wills, from any great calamity that may have fallen on their persons, for they look on it as the height of cruelty and treachery to abandon either of the married persons when they need most the tender care of their consort, and that chiefly in the case of old age, which, as it carries many diseases along with it, so it is a disease of itself.

'But it frequently falls out that when a married couple do not well agree, they, by mutual consent, separate, and find out other persons with whom they hope they may live more happily; yet this is not done without obtaining leave of the Senate, which never admits of a divorce but upon a strict inquiry made, both by the senators and their wives, into the grounds upon which it is desired, and even when they are satisfied concerning the reasons of it they go on but slowly, for they imagine that too great easiness in granting leave for new marriages would very much shake the kindness of married people.

'They punish severely those that defile the marriage bed; if both parties are married they are divorced, and the injured persons may marry one another, or whom they please, but the adulterer and the adulteress are condemned to slavery, yet if either of the injured persons cannot shake off the love of the married person they may live with them still in that state, but they must follow them to that labour to which the slaves are condemned, and sometimes the repentance of the condemned, together with the unshaken kindness of the innocent and injured person, has prevailed so far with the Prince that he has taken off the sentence; but those that relapse after they are once pardoned are punished with death.

'Their law does not determine the punishment for other crimes, but that is left to the Senate, to temper it according to the circumstances of the fact. Husbands have power to correct their wives and parents to chastise their children, unless the fault is so great that a public punishment is thought necessary for striking terror into others. For the most part slavery is the punishment even of the greatest crimes, for as that is no less terrible to the criminals themselves than death, so they think the preserving them in a state of servitude is more for the interest of the commonwealth than killing them, since, as their labour is a greater benefit to the public than their death could be, so the sight of their misery is a more lasting terror to other men than that which would be given by their death. If their slaves rebel, and will not bear their yoke and submit to the labour that is enjoined them, they are treated as wild beasts that cannot be kept in order, neither by a prison nor by their chains, and are at last put to death. But those who bear their punishment patiently, and are so much wrought on by that pressure that lies so hard on them, that it appears they are really more troubled for the crimes they have committed than for the miseries they suffer, are not out of hope, but that, at last, either the Prince will, by his prerogative, or the people, by their intercession, restore them again to their liberty, or, at least, very much mitigate their slavery.

'He that tempts a married woman to adultery is no less severely punished than he that commits it, for they believe that a deliberate design to commit a crime is equal to the fact itself, since its not taking effect does not make the person that miscarried in his attempt at all the less guilty.

'They take great pleasure in fools, and as it is thought a base and unbecoming thing to use them ill, so they do not think it amiss for people to divert themselves with their folly; and, in their opinion, this is a great advantage to the fools themselves; for if men were so sullen and severe as not at all to please themselves with their ridiculous behaviour and foolish sayings, which is all that they can do to recommend themselves to others, it could not be expected that they would be so well provided for nor so tenderly used as they must otherwise be.

'If any man should reproach another for his being misshaped or imperfect in any part of his body, it would not at all be thought a reflection on the person so treated, but it would be accounted scandalous in him that had upbraided another with what he could not help. It is thought a sign of a sluggish and sordid mind not to preserve carefully one's natural beauty; but it is likewise infamous among them to use paint. They all see that no beauty recommends a wife so much to her husband as the probity of her life and her obedience; for as some few are caught and held only by beauty, so all are attracted by the other excellences which charm all the world.

'As they frighten from committing crimes by punishments, so they invite them to the love of virtue by public honours; therefore they erect statues to the memories of such worthy men as have deserved well of their country, and set these in their market-places, both to perpetuate the remembrance of their actions and to be an incitement to their posterity to follow their example.

'If any man aspires to any office he is sure never to compass it. They all live easily together, for none of the magistrates are either insolent or cruel to the people; they affect rather to be called fathers, and, by being really so, they well deserve the name; and the people pay them all the marks of honour the more freely because none are exacted from them. The Prince himself has no distinction, either of garments or of a crown; but is only distinguished by a sheaf of corn carried before him; as the High Priest is also known by his being preceded by a person carrying a wax light.

'They have but few laws, and such is their constitution that they need not many. They very much condemn other nations whose laws, together with the commentaries on them, swell up to so many volumes; for they think it an unreasonable thing to oblige men to obey a body of laws that are both of such a bulk, and so dark as not to be read and understood by every one of the subjects.

'They have no lawyers among them, for they consider them as a sort of people whose profession it is to disguise matters and to wrest the laws, and, therefore, they think it is much better that every man should plead his own cause, and trust it to the judge, as in other places the client trusts it to a counsellor; by this means they both cut off many delays and find out truth more certainly; for after the parties have laid open the merits of the cause, without those artifices which lawyers are apt to suggest, the judge examines the whole matter, and supports the simplicity of such well-meaning persons, whom otherwise crafty men would be sure to run down; and thus they avoid those evils which appear very remarkably among all those nations that labour under a vast load of laws.

'Every one of them is skilled in their law; for, as it is a very short study, so the plainest meaning of which words are capable is always the sense of their laws; and they argue thus: all laws are promulgated for this end, that every man may know his duty; and, therefore, the plainest and most obvious sense of the words is that which ought to be put upon them, since a more refined exposition cannot be easily comprehended, and would only serve to make the laws become useless to the greater part of mankind, and especially to those who need most the direction of them; for it is all one not to make a law at all or to couch it in such terms that, without a quick apprehension and much study, a man cannot find out the true meaning of it, since the generality of mankind are both so dull, and so much employed in their several trades, that they have neither the leisure nor the capacity requisite for such an inquiry.

'Some of their neighbours, who are masters of their own liberties (having long ago, by the assistance of the Utopians, shaken off the yoke of tyranny, and being much taken with those virtues which they observe among them), have come to desire that they would send magistrates to govern them, some changing them every year, and others every five years; at the end of their government they bring them back to Utopia, with great expressions of honour and esteem, and carry away others to govern in their stead. In this they seem to have fallen upon a very good expedient for their own happiness and safety; for since the good or ill condition of a nation depends so much upon their magistrates, they could not have made a better choice than by pitching on men whom no advantages can bias; for wealth is of no use to them, since they must so soon go back to their own country, and they, being strangers among them, are not engaged in any of their heats or animosities; and it is certain that when public judicatories are swayed, either by avarice or partial affections, there must follow a dissolution of justice, the chief sinew of society.

'The Utopians call those nations that come and ask magistrates from them Neighbours; but those to whom they have been of more particular service, Friends; and as all other nations are perpetually either making leagues or breaking them, they never enter into an alliance with any state. They think leagues are useless things, and believe that if the common ties of humanity do not knit men together, the faith of promises will have no great effect; and they are the more confirmed in this by what they see among the nations round about them, who are no strict observers of leagues and treaties.

'We know how religiously they are observed in Europe, more particularly where the Christian doctrine is received, among whom they are sacred and inviolable! – which is partly owing to the justice and goodness of the princes themselves, and partly to the reverence they pay to the popes, who, as they are the most religious observers of their own promises, so they exhort all other princes to perform theirs, and, when fainter methods do not prevail, they compel them to it by the severity of the pastoral censure, and think that it would be the most indecent thing possible if men who are particularly distinguished by the title of "The Faithful" should not religiously keep the faith of their treaties.

'But in that new-found world, which is not more distant from us in situation than the people are in their manners and course of life, there is no trusting to leagues, even though they were made with all the pomp of the most sacred ceremonies; on the contrary, they are on this account the sooner broken, some slight pretence being found in the words of the treaties, which are purposely couched in such ambiguous terms that they can never be so strictly bound but they will always find some loophole to escape at, and thus they break both their leagues and their faith; and this is done with such impudence, that those very men who value themselves on having suggested these expedients to their princes would, with a haughty scorn, declaim against such craft; or, to speak plainer, such fraud and deceit, if they found private men make use of it in their bargains, and would readily say that they deserved to be hanged.

'By this means it is that all sort of justice passes in the world for a low-spirited and vulgar virtue, far below the dignity of royal greatness – or at least there are set up two sorts of justice; the one is mean and creeps on the ground, and, therefore, becomes none but the lower part of mankind, and so must be kept in severely by many restraints, that it may not break out beyond the bounds that are set to it; the other is the peculiar virtue of princes, which, as it is more majestic than that which becomes the rabble, so takes a freer compass, and thus lawful and unlawful are only measured by pleasure and interest. These practices of the princes that lie about Utopia, who make so little account of their faith, seem to be the reasons that determine them to engage in no confederacy. Perhaps they would change their mind if they lived among us; but yet, though treaties were more religiously observed, they would still dislike the custom of making them, since the world has taken up a false maxim upon it, as if there were no tie of nature uniting one nation to another, only separated perhaps by a mountain or a river, and that all were born in a state of hostility, and so might lawfully do all that mischief to their neighbours against which there is no provision made by treaties; and that when treaties are made they do not cut off the enmity or restrain the licence of preying upon each other, if, by the unskilfulness of wording them, there are not effectual provisions made against them; they, on the other hand, judge that no man is to be esteemed our enemy that has never injured us, and that the partnership of human nature is instead of a league; and that kindness and good nature unite men more effectually and with greater strength than any agreements whatsoever, since thereby the engagements of men's hearts become stronger than the bond and obligation of words.

Of Their Military Discipline

'They detest war as a very brutal thing, and which, to the reproach of human nature, is more practised by men than by any sort of beasts. They, in opposition to the sentiments of almost all other nations, think that there is nothing more inglorious than that glory that is gained by war; and therefore, though they accustom themselves daily to military exercises and the discipline of war, in which not only their men, but their women likewise, are trained up, that, in cases of necessity, they may not be quite useless, yet they do not rashly engage in war, unless it be either to defend themselves or their friends from any unjust aggressors, or, out of good nature or in compassion, assist an oppressed nation in shaking off the yoke of tyranny. They, indeed, help their friends not only in defensive but also in offensive wars; but they never do that unless they had been consulted before the breach was made, and, being satisfied with the grounds on which they went, they had found that all demands of reparation were rejected, so that a war was unavoidable.

'This they think to be not only just when one neighbour makes an inroad on another by public order, and carries away the spoils, but when the merchants of one country are oppressed in another, either under pretence of some unjust laws, or by the perverse wresting of good ones. This they count a juster cause of war than the other, because those injuries are done under some colour of laws.

'This was the only ground of that war in which they engaged with the Nephelogetes against the Aleopolitanes, a little before our time; for the merchants of the former having, as they thought, met with great injustice among the latter, which (whether it was in itself right or wrong) drew on a terrible war, in which many of their neighbours were engaged; and their keenness in carrying it on being supported by their strength in maintaining it, it not only shook some very flourishing states and very much afflicted others, but, after a series of much mischief ended in the entire conquest and slavery of the Aleopolitanes, who, though before the war they were in all respects much superior to the Nephelogetes, were yet subdued; but, though the Utopians had assisted them in the war, yet they pretended to no share of the spoil.

'But, though they so vigorously assist their friends in obtaining reparation for the injuries they have received in affairs of this nature, yet, if any such frauds were committed against themselves, provided no violence was done to their persons, they would only, on their being refused satisfaction, forbear trading with such a people. This is not because they consider their neighbours more than their own citizens; but, since their neighbours trade every one upon his own stock, fraud is a more sensible injury to them than it is to the Utopians, among whom the public, in such a case, only suffers, as they expect no thing in return for the merchandise they export but that in which they so much abound, and is of little use to them, the loss does not much affect them. They think, therefore, it would be too severe to revenge a loss attended with so little inconvenience, either to their lives or their subsistence, with the death of many persons; but if any of their people are either killed or wounded wrongfully, whether it be done by public authority, or only by private men, as soon as they hear of it they send ambassadors, and demand that the guilty persons may be delivered up to them, and if that is denied, they declare war; but if it be complied with, the offenders are condemned either to death or slavery.

'They would be both troubled and ashamed of a bloody victory over their enemies; and think it would be as foolish a purchase as to buy the most valuable goods at too high a rate. And in no victory do they glory so much as in that which is gained by dexterity and good conduct without bloodshed. In such cases they appoint public triumphs, and erect trophies to the honour of those who have succeeded; for then do they reckon that a man acts suitably to his nature, when he conquers his enemy in such a way as that no other creature but a man could be capable of, and that is by the strength of his understanding. Bears, lions, boars, wolves, and dogs, and all other animals, employ their bodily force one against another, in which, as many of them are superior to men, both in strength and fierceness, so they are all subdued by his reason and understanding.

'The only design of the Utopians in war is to obtain that by force which, if it had been granted them in time, would have prevented the war; or, if that cannot be done, to take so severe a revenge on those that have injured them that they may be terrified from doing the like for the time to come. By these ends they measure all their designs, and manage them so, that it is visible that the appetite of fame or vainglory does not work so much on there as a just care of their own security.

'As soon as they declare war, they take care to have a great many proclamations, that are marked with their common seal, affixed in the most conspicuous places of their enemies' country. This is carried secretly, and done in many places all at once. In these they promise great rewards to such as shall kill the prince, and lesser in proportion to such as shall kill any other persons who are those on whom, next to the prince himself, they cast the chief balance of the war. And they double the sum to him that, instead of killing the person so marked out, shall take him alive, and put him in their hands. They offer not only indemnity, but rewards, to such of the persons themselves that are so marked, if they will act against their countrymen. By this means those that are named in their schedules become not only distrustful of their fellow citizens, but are jealous of one another, and are much distracted by fear and danger; for it has often fallen out that many of them, and even the prince himself, have been betrayed, by those in whom they have trusted most; for the rewards that the Utopians offer are so immeasurably great, that there is no sort of crime to which men cannot be drawn by them. They consider the risk that those run who undertake such services, and offer a recompense proportioned to the danger – not only a vast deal of gold, but great revenues in lands, that lie among other nations that are their friends, where they may go and enjoy them very securely; and they observe the promises they make of their kind most religiously.

'They very much approve of this way of corrupting their enemies, though it appears to others to be base and cruel; but they look on it as a wise course, to make an end of what would be otherwise a long war, without so much as hazarding one battle to decide it. They think it likewise an act of mercy and love to mankind to prevent the great slaughter of those that must otherwise be killed in the progress of the war, both on their own side and on that of their enemies, by the death of a few that are most guilty; and that in so doing they are kind even to their enemies, and pity them no less than their own people, as knowing that the greater part of them do not engage in the war of their own accord, but are driven into it by the passions of their prince.

'If this method does not succeed with them, then they sow seeds of contention among their enemies, and animate the prince's brother, or some of the nobility, to aspire to the crown. If they cannot disunite them by domestic broils, then they engage their neighbours against them, and make them set on foot some old pretensions, which are never wanting to princes when they have occasion for them. These they plentifully supply with money, though but very sparingly with any auxiliary troops; for they are so tender of their own people that they would not willingly exchange one of them, even with the prince of their enemies' country.

'But as they keep their gold and silver only for such an occasion, so, when that offers itself, they easily part with it; since it would be no convenience to them, though they should reserve nothing of it to themselves. For besides the wealth that they have among them at home, they have a vast treasure abroad; many nations round about them being deep in their debt: so that they hire soldiers from all places for carrying on their wars; but chiefly from the Zapolets, who live five hundred miles east of Utopia. They are a rude, wild, and fierce nation, who delight in the woods and rocks, among which they were born and bred up. They are hardened both against heat, cold, and labour, and know nothing of the delicacies of life. They do not apply themselves to agriculture, nor do they care either for their houses or their clothes: cattle is all that they look after; and for the greatest part they live either by hunting or upon rapine; and are made, as it were, only for war.

'They watch all opportunities of engaging in it, and very readily embrace such as are offered them. Great numbers of them will frequently go out, and offer themselves for a very low pay, to serve any that will employ them: they know none of the arts of life, but those that lead to the taking it away; they serve those that hire them, both with much courage and great fidelity; but will not engage to serve for any determined time, and agree upon such terms, that the next day they may go over to the enemies of those whom they serve if they offer them a greater encouragement; and will, perhaps, return to them the day after that upon a higher advance of their pay. There are few wars in which they make not a considerable part of the armies of both sides: so it often falls out that they who are related, and were hired in the same country, and so have lived long and familiarly together, forgetting both their relations and former friendship, kill one another upon no other consideration than that of being hired to it for a little money by princes of different interests; and such a regard have they for money that they are easily wrought on by the difference of one penny a day to change sides. So entirely does their avarice influence them; and yet this money, which they value so highly, is of little use to them; for what they purchase thus with their blood they quickly waste on luxury, which among them is but of a poor and miserable form.

'This nation serves the Utopians against all people whatsoever, for they pay higher than any other. The Utopians hold this for a maxim, that as they seek out the best sort of men for their own use at home, so they make use of this worst sort of men for the consumption of war; and therefore they hire them with the offers of vast rewards to expose themselves to all sorts of hazards, out of which the greater part never returns to claim their promises; yet they make them good most religiously to such as escape. This animates them to adventure again, whenever there is occasion for it; for the Utopians are not at all troubled how many of these happen to be killed, and reckon it a service done to mankind if they could be a means to deliver the world from such a lewd and vicious sort of people, that seem to have run together, as to the drain of human nature.

'Next to these, they are served in their wars with those upon whose account they undertake them, and with the auxiliary troops of their other friends, to whom they join a few of their own people, and send some man of eminent and approved virtue to command in chief. There are two sent with him, who, during his command, are but private men, but the first is to succeed him if he should happen to be either killed or taken; and, in case of the like misfortune to him, the third comes in his place; and thus they provide against all events, that such accidents as may befall their generals may not endanger their armies.

'When they draw out troops of their own people, they take such out of every city as freely offer themselves, for none are forced to go against their wills, since they think that if any man is pressed that wants courage, he will not only act faintly, but by his cowardice dishearten others. But if an invasion is made on their country, they make use of such men, if they have good bodies, though they are not brave; and either put them aboard their ships, or place them on the walls of their towns, that being so posted, they may find no opportunity of flying away; and thus either shame, the heat of action, or the impossibility of flying, bears down their cowardice; they often make a virtue of necessity, and behave themselves well, because nothing else is left them.

'But as they force no man to go into any foreign war against his will, so they do not hinder those women who are willing to go along with their husbands; on the contrary, they encourage and praise them, and they stand often next their husbands in the front of the army. They also place together those who are related, parents, and children, kindred, and those that are mutually allied, near one another; that those whom nature has inspired with the greatest zeal for assisting one another may be the nearest and readiest to do it; and it is matter of great reproach if husband or wife survive one another, or if a child survives his parent, and therefore when they come to be engaged in action, they continue to fight to the last man, if their enemies stand before them: and as they use all prudent methods to avoid the endangering their own men, and if it is possible let all the action and danger fall upon the troops that they hire, so if it becomes necessary for themselves to engage, they then charge with as much courage as they avoided it before with prudence: nor is it a fierce charge at first, but it increases by degrees; and as they continue in action, they grow more obstinate, and press harder upon the enemy, insomuch that they will much sooner die than give ground; for the certainty that their children will be well looked after when they are dead frees them from all that anxiety concerning them which often masters men of great courage; and thus they are animated by a noble and invincible resolution. Their skill in military affairs increases their courage: and the wise sentiments which, according to the laws of their country, are instilled into them in their education, give additional vigour to their minds: for as they do not undervalue life so as prodigally to throw it away, they are not so indecently fond of it as to preserve it by base and unbecoming methods.

'In the greatest heat of action the bravest of their youth, who have devoted themselves to that service, single out the general of their enemies, set on him either openly or by ambush; pursue him everywhere, and when spent and wearied out, are relieved by others, who never give over the pursuit, either attacking him with close weapons when they can get near him, or with those which wound at a distance, when others get in between them. So that, unless he secures himself by flight, they seldom fail at last to kill or to take him prisoner.

'When they have obtained a victory, they kill as few as possible, and are much more bent on taking many prisoners than on killing those that fly before them. Nor do they ever let their men so loose in the pursuit of their enemies as not to retain an entire body still in order; so that if they have been forced to engage the last of their battalions before they could gain the day, they will rather let their enemies all escape than pursue them when their own army is in disorder; remembering well what has often fallen out to themselves, that when the main body of their army has been quite defeated and broken, when their enemies, imagining the victory obtained, have let themselves loose into an irregular pursuit, a few of them that lay for a reserve, waiting a fit opportunity, have fallen on them in their chase, and when straggling in disorder, and apprehensive of no danger, but counting the day their own, have turned the whole action, and, wresting out of their hands a victory that seemed certain and undoubted, while the vanquished have suddenly become victorious.

'It is hard to tell whether they are more dexterous in laying or avoiding ambushes. They sometimes seem to fly when it is far from their thoughts; and when they intend to give ground, they do it so that it is very hard to find out their design. If they see they are ill posted, or are like to be overpowered by numbers, they then either march off in the night with great silence, or by some stratagem delude their enemies. If they retire in the day-time, they do it in such order that it is no less dangerous to fall upon them in a retreat than in a march. They fortify their camps with a deep and large trench; and throw up the earth that is dug out of it for a wall; nor do they employ only their slaves in this, but the whole army works at it, except those that are then upon the guard; so that when so many hands are at work, a great line and a strong fortification is finished in so short a time that it is scarce credible.

'Their armour is very strong for defence, and yet is not so heavy as to make them uneasy in their marches; they can even swim with it. All that are trained up to war practise swimming. Both horse and foot make great use of arrows, and are very expert. They have no swords, but fight with a pole-axe that is both sharp and heavy, by which they thrust or strike down an enemy. They are very good at finding out warlike machines, and disguise them so well that the enemy does not perceive them till he feels the use of them; so that he cannot prepare such a defence as would render them useless; the chief consideration had in the making them is that they may be easily carried and managed.

'If they agree to a truce, they observe it so religiously that no provocations will make them break it. They never lay their enemies' country waste nor burn their corn, and even in their marches they take all possible care that neither horse nor foot may tread it down, for they do not know but that they may have use for it themselves. They hurt no man whom they find disarmed, unless he is a spy. When a town is surrendered to them, they take it into their protection; and when they carry a place by storm they never plunder it, but put those only to the sword that oppose the rendering of it up, and make the rest of the garrison slaves, but for the other inhabitants, they do them no hurt; and if any of them had advised a surrender, they give them good rewards out of the estates of those that they condemn, and distribute the rest among their auxiliary troops, but they themselves take no share of the spoil.

'When a war is ended, they do not oblige their friends to reimburse their expenses; but they obtain them of the conquered, either in money, which they keep for the next occasion, or in lands, out of which a constant revenue is to be paid them; by many increases the revenue which they draw out from several countries on such occasions is now risen to above 700,000 ducats a year. They send some of their own people to receive these revenues, who have orders to live magnificently and like princes, by which means they consume much of it upon the place; and either bring over the rest to Utopia or lend it to that nation in which it lies. This they most commonly do, unless some great occasion, which falls out but very seldom, should oblige them to call for it all. It is out of these lands that they assign rewards to such as they encourage to adventure on desperate attempts. If any prince that engages in war with them is making preparations for invading their country, they prevent him, and make his country the seat of the war; for they do not willingly suffer any war to break in upon their island; and if that should happen, they would only defend themselves by their own people; but would not call for auxiliary troops to their assistance.

Of the Religions of the Utopians

'There are several sorts of religions, not only in different parts of the island, but even in every town; some worshipping the sun, others the moon or one of the planets. Some worship such men as have been eminent in former times for virtue or glory, not only as ordinary deities, but as the supreme god. Yet the greater and wiser sort of them worship none of these, but adore one eternal, invisible, infinite, and incomprehensible Deity; as a Being that is far above all our apprehensions, that is spread over the whole universe, not by His bulk, but by His power and virtue; Him they call the Father of All, and acknowledge that the beginnings, the increase, the progress, the vicissitudes, and the end of all things come only from Him; nor do they offer divine honours to any but to Him alone.

'And, indeed, though they differ concerning other things, yet all agree in this: that they think there is one Supreme Being that made and governs the world, whom they call, in the language of their country, Mithras. They differ in this: that one thinks the god whom he worships is this Supreme Being, and another thinks that his idol is that god; but they all agree in one principle, that whoever is this Supreme Being, He is also that great essence to whose glory and majesty all honours are ascribed by the consent of all nations.

'By degrees they fall off from the various superstitions that are among them, and grow up to that one religion that is the best and most in request; and there is no doubt to be made, but that all the others had vanished long ago, if some of those who advised them to lay aside their superstitions had not met with some unhappy accidents, which, being considered as inflicted by heaven, made them afraid that the god whose worship had like to have been abandoned had interposed and revenged themselves on those who despised their authority.

'After they had heard from us an account of the doctrine, the course of life, and the miracles of Christ, and of the wonderful constancy of so many martyrs, whose blood, so willingly offered up by them, was the chief occasion of spreading their religion over a vast number of nations, it is not to be imagined how inclined they were to receive it. I shall not determine whether this proceeded from any secret inspiration of God, or whether it was because it seemed so favourable to that community of goods, which is an opinion so particular as well as so dear to them; since they perceived that Christ and His followers lived by that rule, and that it was still kept up in some communities among the sincerest sort of Christians. From whichsoever of these motives it might be, true it is, that many of them came over to our religion, and were initiated into it by baptism. But as two of our number were dead, so none of the four that survived were in priests' orders, we, therefore, could only baptize them, so that, to our great regret, they could not partake of the other sacraments, that can only be administered by priests, but they are instructed concerning them and long most vehemently for them. They have had great disputes among themselves, whether one chosen by them to be a priest would not be thereby qualified to do all the things that belong to that character, even though he had no authority derived from the Pope, and they seemed to be resolved to choose some for that employment, but they had not done it when I left them.

'Those among them that have not received our religion do not fright any from it, and use none ill that goes over to it, so that all the while I was there one man was only punished on this occasion. He being newly baptized did, notwithstanding all that we could say to the contrary, dispute publicly concerning the Christian religion, with more zeal than discretion, and with so much heat, that he not only preferred our worship to theirs, but condemned all their rites as profane, and cried out against all that adhered to them as impious and sacrilegious persons, that were to be damned to everlasting burnings. Upon his having frequently preached in this manner he was seized, and after trial he was condemned to banishment, not for having disparaged their religion, but for his inflaming the people to sedition; for this is one of their most ancient laws, that no man ought to be punished for his religion.

'At the first constitution of their government, Utopus having understood that before his coming among them the old inhabitants had been engaged in great quarrels concerning religion, by which they were so divided among themselves, that he found it an easy thing to conquer them, since, instead of uniting their forces against him, every different party in religion fought by themselves. After he had subdued them he made a law that every man might be of what religion he pleased, and might endeavour to draw others to it by the force of argument and by amicable and modest ways, but without bitterness against those of other opinions; but that he ought to use no other force but that of persuasion, and was neither to mix with it reproaches nor violence; and such as did otherwise were to be condemned to banishment or slavery.

'This law was made by Utopus, not only for preserving the public peace, which he saw suffered much by daily contentions and irreconcilable heats, but because he thought the interest of religion itself required it. He judged it not fit to determine anything rashly; and seemed to doubt whether those different forms of religion might not all come from God, who might inspire man in a different manner, and be pleased with this variety; he therefore thought it indecent and foolish for any man to threaten and terrify another to make him believe what did not appear to him to be true. And supposing that only one religion was really true, and the rest false, he imagined that the native force of truth would at last break forth and shine bright, if supported only by the strength of argument, and attended to with a gentle and unprejudiced mind; while, on the other hand, if such debates were carried on with violence and tumults, as the most wicked are always the most obstinate, so the best and most holy religion might be choked with superstition, as corn is with briars and thorns; he therefore left men wholly to their liberty, that they might be free to believe as they should see cause; only he made a solemn and severe law against such as should so far degenerate from the dignity of human nature, as to think that our souls died with our bodies, or that the world was governed by chance, without a wise overruling Providence: for they all formerly believed that there was a state of rewards and punishments to the good and bad after this life; and they now look on those that think otherwise as scarce fit to be counted men, since they degrade so noble a being as the soul, and reckon it no better than a beast's: thus they are far from looking on such men as fit for human society, or to be citizens of a well-ordered commonwealth; since a man of such principles must needs, as oft as he dares do it, despise all their laws and customs: for there is no doubt to be made, that a man who is afraid of nothing but the law, and apprehends nothing after death, will not scruple to break through all the laws of his country, either by fraud or force, when by this means he may satisfy his appetites. They never raise any that hold these maxims, either to honours or offices, nor employ them in any public trust, but despise them, as men of base and sordid minds. Yet they do not punish them, because they lay this down as a maxim, that a man cannot make himself believe anything he pleases; nor do they drive any to dissemble their thoughts by threatenings, so that men are not tempted to lie or disguise their opinions; which being a sort of fraud, is abhorred by the Utopians: they take care indeed to prevent their disputing in defence of these opinions, especially before the common people: but they suffer, and even encourage them to dispute concerning them in private with their priest, and other grave men, being confident that they will be cured of those mad opinions by having reason laid before them. There are many among them that run far to the other extreme, though it is neither thought an ill nor unreasonable opinion, and therefore is not at all discouraged. They think that the souls of beasts are immortal, though far inferior to the dignity of the human soul, and not capable of so great a happiness.

'They are almost all of them very firmly persuaded that good men will be infinitely happy in another state: so that though they are compassionate to all that are sick, yet they lament no man's death, except they see him loath to part with life; for they look on this as a very ill presage, as if the soul, conscious to itself of guilt, and quite hopeless, was afraid to leave the body, from some secret hints of approaching misery. They think that such a man's appearance before God cannot be acceptable to Him, who being called on, does not go out cheerfully, but is backward and unwilling, and is as it were dragged to it. They are struck with horror when they see any die in this manner, and carry them out in silence and with sorrow, and praying God that He would be merciful to the errors of the departed soul, they lay the body in the ground: but when any die cheerfully, and full of hope, they do not mourn for them, but sing hymns when they carry out their bodies, and commending their souls very earnestly to God: their whole behaviour is then rather grave than sad, they burn the body, and set up a pillar where the pile was made, with an inscription to the honour of the deceased.

When they come from the funeral, they discourse of his good life, and worthy actions, but speak of nothing oftener and with more pleasure than of his serenity at the hour of death.

'They think such respect paid to the memory of good men is both the greatest incitement to engage others to follow their example, and the most acceptable worship that can be offered them; for they believe that though by the imperfection of human sight they are invisible to us, yet they are present among us, and hear those discourses that pass concerning themselves. They believe it inconsistent with the happiness of departed souls not to be at liberty to be where they will: and do not imagine them capable of the ingratitude of not desiring to see those friends with whom they lived on earth in the strictest bonds of love and kindness: besides, they are persuaded that good men, after death, have these affections; and all other good dispositions increased rather than diminished, and therefore conclude that they are still among the living, and observe all they say or do. From hence they engage in all their affairs with the greater confidence of success, as trusting to their protection; while this opinion of the presence of their ancestors is a restraint that prevents their engaging in ill designs.

'They despise and laugh at auguries, and the other vain and superstitious ways of divination, so much observed among other nations; but have great reverence for such miracles as cannot flow from any of the powers of nature, and look on them as effects and indications of the presence of the Supreme Being, of which they say many instances have occurred among them; and that sometimes their public prayers, which upon great and dangerous occasions they have solemnly put up to God, with assured confidence of being heard, have been answered in a miraculous manner.

'They think the contemplating God in His works, and the adoring Him for them, is a very acceptable piece of worship to Him.

'There are many among them that upon a motive of religion neglect learning, and apply themselves to no sort of study; nor do they allow themselves any leisure time, but are perpetually employed, believing that by the good things that a man does he secures to himself that happiness that comes after death. Some of these visit the sick; others mend highways, cleanse ditches, repair bridges, or dig turf, gravel, or stone. Others fell and cleave timber, and bring wood, corn, and other necessaries, on carts, into their towns; nor do these only serve the public, but they serve even private men, more than the slaves themselves do: for if there is anywhere a rough, hard, and sordid piece of work to be done, from which many are frightened by the labour and loathsomeness of it, if not the despair of accomplishing it, they cheerfully, and of their own accord, take that to their share; and by that means, as they ease others very much, so they afflict themselves, and spend their whole life in hard labour: and yet they do not value themselves upon this, nor lessen other people's credit to raise their own; but by their stooping to such servile employments they are so far from being despised, that they are so much the more esteemed by the whole nation.

'Of these there are two sorts: some live unmarried and chaste, and abstain from eating any sort of flesh; and thus weaning themselves from all the pleasures of the present life, which they account hurtful, they pursue, even by the hardest and painfullest methods possible, that blessedness which they hope for hereafter; and the nearer they approach to it, they are the more cheerful and earnest in their endeavours after it. Another sort of them is less willing to put themselves to much toil, and therefore prefer a married state to a single one; and as they do not deny themselves the pleasure of it, so they think the begetting of children is a debt which they owe to human nature, and to their country; nor do they avoid any pleasure that does not hinder labour; and therefore eat flesh so much the more willingly, as they find that by this means they are the more able to work: the Utopians look upon these as the wiser sect, but they esteem the others as the most holy. They would indeed laugh at any man who, from the principles of reason, would prefer an unmarried state to a married, or a life of labour to an easy life: but they reverence and admire such as do it from the motives of religion. There is nothing in which they are more cautious than in giving their opinion positively concerning any sort of religion. The men that lead those severe lives are called in the language of their country Brutheskas, which answers to those we call Religious Orders.

'Their priests are men of eminent piety, and therefore they are but few, for there are only thirteen in every town, one for every temple; but when they go to war, seven of these go out with their forces, and seven others are chosen to supply their room in their absence; but these enter again upon their employments when they return; and those who served in their absence, attend upon the high priest, till vacancies fall by death; for there is one set over the rest. They are chosen by the people as the other magistrates are, by suffrages given in secret, for preventing of factions: and when they are chosen, they are consecrated by the college of priests.

'The care of all sacred things, the worship of God, and an inspection into the manners of the people, are committed to them. It is a reproach to a man to be sent for by any of them, or for them to speak to him in secret, for that always gives some suspicion: all that is incumbent on them is only to exhort and admonish the people; for the power of correcting and punishing ill men belongs wholly to the Prince, and to the other magistrates: the severest thing that the priest does is the excluding those that are desperately wicked from joining in their worship: there is not any sort of punishment more dreaded by them than this, for as it loads them with infamy, so it fills them with secret horrors, such is their reverence to their religion; nor will their bodies be long exempted from their share of trouble; for if they do not very quickly satisfy the priests of the truth of their repentance, they are seized on by the Senate, and punished for their impiety.

'The education of youth belongs to the priests, yet they do not take so much care of instructing them in letters, as in forming their minds and manners aright; they use all possible methods to infuse, very early, into the tender and flexible minds of children, such opinions as are both good in themselves and will be useful to their country, for when deep impressions of these things are made at that age, they follow men through the whole course of their lives, and conduce much to preserve the peace of the government, which suffers by nothing more than by vices that rise out of ill opinions.

'The wives of their priests are the most extraordinary women of the whole country; sometimes the women themselves are made priests, though that falls out but seldom, nor are any but ancient widows chosen into that order.

'None of the magistrates have greater honour paid them than is paid the priests; and if they should happen to commit any crime, they would not be questioned for it; their punishment is left to God, and to their own consciences; for they do not think it lawful to lay hands on any man, how wicked soever he is, that has been in a peculiar manner dedicated to God; nor do they find any great inconvenience in this, both because they have so few priests, and because these are chosen with much caution, so that it must be a very unusual thing to find one who, merely out of regard to his virtue, and for his being esteemed a singularly good man, was raised up to so great a dignity, degenerate into corruption and vice; and if such a thing should fall out, for man is a changeable creature, yet, there being few priests, and these having no authority but what rises out of the respect that is paid them, nothing of great consequence to the public can proceed from the indemnity that the priests enjoy.

'They have, indeed, very few of them, lest greater numbers sharing in the same honour might make the dignity of that order, which they esteem so highly, to sink in its reputation; they also think it difficult to find out many of such an exalted pitch of goodness as to be equal to that dignity, which demands the exercise of more than ordinary virtues.

'Nor are the priests in greater veneration among them than they are among their neighbouring nations, as you may imagine by that which I think gives occasion for it.

'When the Utopians engage in battle, the priests who

accompany them to the war, apparelled in their sacred vestments, kneel down during the action (in a place not far from
the field), and, lifting up their hands to heaven, pray, first for
peace, and then for victory to their own side, and particularly that it may be gained without the effusion of much
blood on either side; and when the victory turns to their
side, they run in among their own men to restrain their fury;
and if any of their enemies see them or call to them, they are
preserved by that means; and such as can come so near them
as to touch their garments have not only their lives, but their
fortunes secured to them; it is upon this account that all the
nations round about consider them so much, and treat them
with such reverence, that they have been often no less able
to preserve their own people from the fury of their enemies
than to save their enemies from their rage; for it has sometimes fallen out, that when their armies have been in disorder and forced to fly, so that their enemies were running
upon the slaughter and spoil, the priests by interposing have
separated them from one another, and stopped the effusion
of more blood; so that, by their mediation, a peace has been
concluded on very reasonable terms; nor is there any nation
about them so fierce, cruel, or barbarous, as not to look upon
their persons as sacred and inviolable.

'The first and the last day of the month, and of the year, is
a festival; they measure their months by the course of the
moon, and their years by the course of the sun: the first days
are called in their language the Cynemernes, and the last the
Trapemernes, which answers in our language, to the festival
that begins or ends the season.

'They have magnificent temples, that are not only nobly
built, but extremely spacious, which is the more necessary as

they have so few of them; they are a little dark within, which proceeds not from any error in the architecture, but is done with design; for their priests think that too much light dissipates the thoughts, and that a more moderate degree of it both recollects the mind and raises devotion.

'Though there are many different forms of religion among them, yet all these, how various soever, agree in the main point, which is the worshipping the Divine Essence; and, therefore, there is nothing to be seen or heard in their temples in which the several persuasions among them may not agree; for every sect performs those rites that are peculiar to it in their private houses, nor is there anything in the public worship that contradicts the particular ways of those different sects. There are no images for God in their temples, so that every one may represent Him to his thoughts according to the way of his religion; nor do they call this one God by any other name but that of Mithras, which is the common name by which they all express the Divine Essence, whatsoever otherwise they think it to be; nor are there any prayers among them but such as every one of them may use without prejudice to his own opinion.

'They meet in their temples on the evening of the festival that concludes a season, and not having yet broke their fast, they thank God for their good success during that year or month which is then at an end; and the next day, being that which begins the new season, they meet early in their temples, to pray for the happy progress of all their affairs during that period upon which they then enter. In the festival which concludes the period, before they go to the temple, both wives and children fall on their knees before their husbands or parents and confess everything in which they have either erred or failed in their duty, and beg pardon for it. Thus all little discontents in families are removed, that they may offer up their devotions with a pure and serene mind; for they hold it a great impiety to enter upon them with disturbed thoughts, or with a consciousness of their bearing hatred or anger in their hearts to any person whatsoever; and think that they should become liable to severe punishments if they presumed to offer sacrifices without cleansing their hearts, and reconciling all their differences.

'In the temples the two sexes are separated, the men go to the right hand, and the women to the left; and the males and females all place themselves before the head and master or mistress of the family to which they belong, so that those who have the government of them at home may see their deportment in public. And they intermingle them so, that the younger and the older may be set by one another; for if the younger sort were all set together, they would, perhaps, trifle away that time too much in which they ought to beget in themselves that religious dread of the Supreme Being which is the greatest and almost the only incitement to virtue.

'They offer up no living creature in sacrifice, nor do they think it suitable to the Divine Being, from whose bounty it is that these creatures have derived their lives, to take pleasure in their deaths, or the offering up their blood. They burn incense and other sweet odours, and have a great number of wax lights during their worship, not out of any imagination that such oblations can add anything to the divine nature (which even prayers cannot do), but as it is a harmless and pure way of worshipping God; so they think those sweet savours and lights, together with some other ceremonies, by a secret and unaccountable virtue, elevate men's souls, and inflame them with greater energy and cheerfulness during the divine worship.

'All the people appear in the temples in white garments; but the priest's vestments are parti-coloured, and both the work and colours are wonderful. They are made of no rich materials, for they are neither embroidered nor set with precious stones; but are composed of the plumes of several birds, laid together with so much art, and so neatly, that the true value of them is far beyond the costliest materials. They say, that in the ordering and placing those plumes some dark mysteries are represented, which pass down among their priests in a secret tradition concerning them; and that they are as hieroglyphics, putting them in mind of the blessing that they have received from God, and of their duties, both to Him and to their neighbours.

'As soon as the priest appears in those ornaments, they all fall prostrate on the ground, with so much reverence and so deep a silence, that such as look on cannot but be struck with it, as if it were the effect of the appearance of a deity. After they have been for some time in this posture, they all stand up, upon a sign given by the priest, and sing hymns to the honour of God, some musical instruments playing all the while. These are quite of another form than those used among us; but, as many of them are much sweeter than ours, so others are made use of by us. Yet in one thing they very much exceed us: all their music, both vocal and instrumental, is adapted to imitate and express the passions, and is so happily suited to every occasion, that, whether the subject of the hymn be cheerful, or formed to soothe or trouble the mind, or to express grief or remorse, the music takes the impression of whatever is represented, affects and kindles the passions, and works the sentiments deep into the hearts of the hearers.

'When this is done, both priests and people offer up very solemn prayers to God in a set form of words; and these are so composed, that whatsoever is pronounced by the whole assembly may be likewise applied by every man in particular to his own condition. In these they acknowledge God to be the author and governor of the world, and the fountain of all the good they receive, and therefore offer up to him their thanksgiving; and, in particular, bless him for His goodness in ordering it so, that they are born under the happiest government in the world, and are of a religion which they hope is the truest of all others; but, if they are mistaken, and if there is either a better government, or a religion more acceptable to God, they implore His goodness to let them know it, vowing that they resolve to follow him whithersoever he leads them; but if their government is the best, and their religion the truest, then they pray that He may fortify them in it, and bring all the world both to the same rules of life, and to the same opinions concerning Himself, unless, according to the unsearchableness of His mind, He is pleased with a variety of religions.

'Then they pray that God may give them an easy passage at last to Himself, not presuming to set limits to Him, how early or late it should be; but, if it may be wished for without derogating from His supreme authority, they desire to be quickly delivered, and to be taken to Himself, though by the most terrible kind of death, rather than to be detained long from seeing Him by the most prosperous course of life. When this prayer is ended, they all fall down again upon the ground; and, after a little while, they rise up, go home to dinner, and spend the rest of the day in diversion or military exercises.

'Thus have I described to you, as particularly as I could, the Constitution of that commonwealth, which I do not only think the best in the world, but indeed the only commonwealth that truly deserves that name.

'In all other places it is visible that, while people talk of a commonwealth, every man only seeks his own wealth; but there, where no man has any property, all men zealously pursue the good of the public, and, indeed, it is no wonder to see men act so differently, for in other commonwealths every man knows that, unless he provides for himself, how flourishing soever the commonwealth may be, he must die of hunger, so that he sees the necessity of preferring his own concerns to the public; but in Utopia, where every man has a right to everything, they all know that if care is taken to keep the public stores full no private man can want anything; for among them there is no unequal distribution, so that no man is poor, none in necessity, and though no man has anything, yet they are all rich; for what can make a man so rich as to lead a serene and cheerful life, free from anxieties; neither apprehending want himself, nor vexed with the endless complaints of his wife? He is not afraid of the misery of his children, nor is he contriving how to raise a portion for his daughters; but is secure in this, that both he and his wife, his children and grand-children, to as many generations as he can fancy, will all live both plentifully and happily; since, among them, there is no less care taken of those who were once engaged in labour, but grow afterwards unable to follow it, than there is, elsewhere, of these that continue still employed.

'I would gladly hear any man compare the justice that is among them with that of all other nations; among whom, may I perish, if I see anything that looks either like justice or equity; for what justice is there in this: that a nobleman, a goldsmith, a banker, or any other man, that either does nothing at all, or, at best, is employed in things that are of no use to the public, should live in great luxury and splendour upon what is so ill acquired, and a mean man, a carter, a smith, or a ploughman, that works harder even than the beasts themselves, and is employed in labours so necessary, that no commonwealth could hold out a year without them, can only earn so poor a livelihood and must lead so miserable a life, that the condition of the beasts is much better than theirs? For as the beasts do not work so constantly, so they feed almost as well, and with more pleasure, and have no anxiety about what is to come, while these men are depressed by a barren and fruitless employment, and tormented with the apprehensions of want in their old age; since that which they get by their daily labour does but maintain them at present, and is consumed as fast as it comes in, there is no surplus left to lay up for old age.

'Is not that government both unjust and ungrateful, that is so prodigal of its favours to those that are called gentlemen, or goldsmiths, or such others who are idle, or live either by flattery or by contriving the arts of vain pleasure, and, on the other hand, takes no care of those of a meaner sort, such as ploughmen, colliers, and smiths, without whom it could not subsist? But after the public has reaped all the advantage of their service, and they come to be oppressed with age, sickness, and want, all their labours and the good they have done is forgotten, and all the recompense given them is that they are left to die in great misery. The richer sort are often endeavouring to bring the hire of labourers lower, not only by their fraudulent practices, but by the laws which they procure to be made to that effect, so that though it is a thing most unjust in itself to give such small rewards to those who deserve so well of the public, yet they have given those hardships the name and colour of justice, by procuring laws to be made for regulating them.

'Therefore I must say that, as I hope for mercy, I can have no other notion of all the other governments that I see or know, than that they are a conspiracy of the rich, who, on pretence of managing the public, only pursue their private ends, and devise all the ways and arts they can find out; first, that they may, without danger, preserve all that they have so ill-acquired, and then, that they may engage the poor to toil and labour for them at as low rates as possible, and oppress them as much as they please; and if they can but prevail to get these contrivances established by the show of public authority, which is considered as the representative of the whole people, then they are accounted laws; yet these wicked men, after they have, by a most insatiable covetousness, divided that among themselves with which all the rest might have been well supplied, are far from that happiness that is enjoyed among the Utopians; for the use as well as the desire of money being extinguished, much anxiety and great occasions of mischief is cut off with it, and who does not see that the frauds, thefts, robberies, quarrels, tumults, contentions, seditions, murders, treacheries, and witchcrafts, which are, indeed, rather punished than restrained by the seventies of law, would all fall off, if money were not any more valued by the world? Men's fears, solicitudes, cares, labours, and watchings would all perish in the same moment with the value of money; even poverty itself, for the relief of which money seems most necessary, would fall. But, in order to the apprehending this aright, take one instance:

'Consider any year, that has been so unfruitful that many thousands have died of hunger; and yet if, at the end of that year, a survey was made of the granaries of all the rich men that have hoarded up the corn, it would be found that there was enough among them to have prevented all that consumption of men that perished in misery; and that, if it had been distributed among them, none would have felt the terrible effects of that scarcity: so easy a thing would it be to supply all the necessities of life, if that blessed thing called money, which is pretended to be invented for procuring them was not really the only thing that obstructed their being procured!

'I do not doubt but rich men are sensible of this, and that they well know how much a greater happiness it is to want nothing necessary, than to abound in many superfluities; and to be rescued out of so much misery, than to abound with so much wealth: and I cannot think but the sense of every man's interest, added to the authority of Christ's commands, who, as He was infinitely wise, knew what was best, and was not less good in discovering it to us, would have drawn all the world over to the laws of the Utopians, if pride, that plague of human nature, that source of so much misery, did not hinder it; for this vice does not measure happiness so much by its own conveniences, as by the miseries of others; and would not be satisfied with being thought a goddess, if none were left that were miserable,

over whom she might insult. Pride thinks its own happiness
shines the brighter, by comparing it with the misfortunes of
other persons; that by displaying its own wealth they may
feel their poverty the more sensibly. This is that infernal
serpent that creeps into the breasts of mortals, and possesses
them too much to be easily drawn out; and, therefore, I am
glad that the Utopians have fallen upon this form of government, in which I wish that all the world could be so wise as
to imitate them; for they have, indeed, laid down such a
scheme and foundation of policy, that as men live happily
under it, so it is like to be of great continuance; for they
having rooted out of the minds of their people all the seeds,
both of ambition and faction, there is no danger of any
commotions at home; which alone has been the ruin of many
states that seemed otherwise to be well secured; but as long
as they live in peace at home, and are governed by such good
laws, the envy of all their neighbouring princes, who have
often, though in vain, attempted their ruin, will never be
able to put their state into any commotion or disorder.'

When Raphael had thus made an end of speaking, though
many things occurred to me, both concerning the manners
and laws of that people, that seemed very absurd, as well in
their way of making war, as in their notions of religion and
divine matters – together with several other particulars, but
chiefly what seemed the foundation of all the rest, their
living in common, without the use of money, by which all
nobility, magnificence, splendour, and majesty, which,
according to the common opinion, are the true ornaments of
a nation, would be quite taken away – yet since I perceived
that Raphael was weary, and was not sure whether he could
easily bear contradiction, remembering that he had taken

notice of some, who seemed to think they were bound in honour to support the credit of their own wisdom, by finding out something to censure in all other men's inventions, besides their own, I only commended their Constitution, and the account he had given of it in general; and so, taking him by the hand, carried him to supper, and told him I would find out some other time for examining this subject more particularly, and for discoursing more copiously upon it. And, indeed, I shall be glad to embrace an opportunity of doing it. In the meanwhile, though it must be confessed that he is both a very learned man and a person who has obtained a great knowledge of the world, I cannot perfectly agree to everything he has related. However, there are many things in the commonwealth of Utopia that I rather wish, than hope, to see followed in our governments.

PART III:
ESSAYS

by Ursula K. Le Guin

1

A Non-Euclidean View of California as a Cold Place to Be

When I planned and wrote my 1974 novel The Dispossessed: An Ambiguous Utopia, *pacifist Anarchist thought was my guidebook, and the essential conception of the book is rational and political, insofar as Anarchism is either. After it was done I began to wish I could go on from it towards, as it were, an even more open utopia.*

In 1982, I wrote this essay to honour the memory of a good friend and a good utopian theorist, and to clarify my thoughts and opinions on the general project of writing utopia. At the time, I wasn't aware that it had a further purpose. I see now that, while decrying the blueprint utopia, the builder's kit for a rationally conceived Good Society, I was groping after the new direction I myself might follow – the way to my own, personal vision of a place where people might have a better chance to live both rightly and well.

In 1985 I published the result of these explorations as a novel, an 'archaeology of the future', Always Coming Home. *The story is set in a Californian valley that I've known all my life and love dearly, the earthquake-shaken, immovable centre of my world. I strove to be absolutely faithful to the nature of that place in the sense of its actual geology, flora, and fauna, and also to my understanding of its nature as holding the potentiality of sacredness. For that reason, writing the novel demanded a greater depth of emotional involvement and degree of experiment and risk than any of my previous books. Often misunderstood as nostalgic or regressive in intent, sometimes dismissed as escapist or mystical,* Always Coming Home *defied utopian expectation in a way* The Dispossessed *does not.*

Is it possible to write a utopia, now, that isn't in the old science-fiction mode, a mere technofix?

Dystopias are certainly easier. At the moment we're flooded with novels grimly revelling in the near-future breakdown of nature and self-destruction of civilisation. Such a collapse appears in Always Coming Home, *but as an historical period – still known, still incalculably damaging, but past. The society there described, aware of its shaky foundations, is less assertive, more introverted than the classic utopian societies, more yin than yang. It draws its inspiration from Lao Tzu as much as from Thomas More. Still, it is an early attempt to carry the great utopian project More began into a new world, beyond the conventions and limitations of the old. I am perfectly sure it will not be the last.*

Robert C. Elliott died in 1981 at the very noon of his scholarship, just after completing his book *The Literary Persona.* He was the truest of teachers, the kindest of friends. This paper was prepared to be read as the first in a series of lectures at his college of the University of California, San Diego, honouring his memory.

We use the French word *lecture*, 'reading', to mean reading and speaking aloud, a performance; the French call such a performance not a *lecture* but a *conference*. The distinction is interesting. Reading is a silent collaboration of reader and writer, apart; lecturing, a noisy collaboration of lecturer and audience, together. The peculiar patchwork form of this paper is my attempt to make it a 'conference', a performable work, a piece for voices. The time and place, a warm April night in La Jolla in 1982, are past, and the warm and noisy audience must be replaced by the gentle reader; but the first voice is still that of Bob Elliott.

In *The Shape of Utopia*, speaking of our modern distrust of utopia, he said,

> If the word is to be redeemed, it will have to be by someone who has followed utopia into the abyss which yawns behind the Grand Inquisitor's vision, and who then has clambered out on the other side.*

That is my starting point, that startling image; and my motto is:

Usà puyew usu wapiw!

We shall be returning to both, never fear; what I am about here is returning.

In the first chapter of *The Shape of Utopia*, Bob points out that in the great participatory festivals such as Saturnalia, Mardi Gras, or Christmas, the age of peace and equality, the Golden Age, may be lived in an interval set apart for it, a

---

* Robert C. Elliott, *The Shape of Utopia* (Chicago: University of Chicago Press, 1970), p. 100.

time outside of daily time. But to bring perfect *communitas* into the structure of ordinary society would be a job only Zeus could handle; or, 'if one does not believe in Zeus's good will, or even in his existence', says Bob, it becomes a job for the mind of man.

Utopia is the application of man's reason and his will to the myth (of the Golden Age), man's effort to work out imaginatively what happens – or might happen – when the primal longings embodied in the myth confront the principle of reality. In this effort man no longer merely dreams of a divine state in some remote time: he assumes the role of creator.*

Now, the Golden Age, or Dream Time, is remote only from the rational mind. It is not accessible to euclidean reason; but on the evidence of all myth and mysticism, and the assurance of every participatory religion, it is, to those with the gift or discipline to perceive it, right here, right now. Whereas it is of the very essence of the rational or Jovian utopia that it is *not* here and *not* now. It is made by the reaction of will and reason against, away from, the here-and-now, and it is, as More said in naming it, nowhere. It is pure structure without content; pure model; goal. That is its virtue. Utopia is uninhabitable. As soon as we reach it, it ceases to be utopia. As evidence of this sad but ineluctable fact, may I point out that we in this room, here and now, are inhabiting utopia.

I was told as a child, and like to believe, that California was named 'The Golden State' not just for the stuff Sutter found but for the wild poppies on its hills and the wild oats of summer. To the Spanish and the Mexicans I gather it was

* Ibid., pp. 8, 9.

the boondocks; but to the Anglos it has been a true utopia: the Golden Age made accessible by willpower, the wild paradise to be tamed by reason; the place where you go free of the old bonds and cramps, leaving behind your farm and your galoshes, casting aside your rheumatism and your inhibitions, taking up a new 'life style' in a not-here-not-now where everybody gets rich quick in the movies or finds the meaning of life, or anyhow gets a good tan hang-gliding. And the wild oats and poppies still come up pure gold in cracks in the cement we have poured over utopia.

In 'assuming the role of the creator' we seek what Lao Tzu calls 'the profit of what is not', rather than participating in what is. To reconstruct the world, to rebuild or rationalize it, is to run the risk of losing or destroying what in fact is.

After all, California was not empty when the Anglos came. Despite the efforts of the missionaries, it was still the most heavily populated region in North America.

What the whites perceived as a wilderness to be 'tamed' was in fact better known to human beings than it has ever been since: known and named. Every hill, every valley, creek, canyon, gulch, gully, draw, point, cliff, bluff, beach, bend, good-sized boulder, and tree of any character had its name, its place in the order of things. An order was perceived, of which the invaders were entirely ignorant. Each of those names named, not a goal, not a place to get to, but a place where one is: a centre of the world. There were centres of the world all over California. One of them is a bluff on the Klamath River. Its name was Katimin. The bluff is still there, but it has no name, and the centre of the world is not there. The six directions can meet only in lived time, in the place people call home, the seventh direction, the centre.

But we leave home, shouting Avanti! and Westward Ho!, driven by our godlike reason, which chafes at the limited, intractable, unreasonable present, and yearns to free itself from the fetters of the past.

'People are always shouting they want to create a better future', says Milan Kundera, in *The Book of Laughter and Forgetting*. 'It's not true. The future is an apathetic void of no interest to anyone. The past is full of life, eager to irritate us, provoke and insult us, tempt us to destroy or repaint it. The only reason people want to be masters of the future is to change the past.'*

And at the end of the book he talks to the interviewer about forgetting: forgetting is

> The great private problem of man: death as the loss of the self. But what is this self? It is the sum of everything we remember. Thus, what terrifies us about death is not the loss of the future but the loss of the past.[†]

And so, Kundera says, when a big power wants to deprive a small one of its national identity, of its self-consciousness, it uses what he calls the 'method of organized forgetting'.

And when a future-oriented culture impinges upon a present-centred one, the method becomes a compulsion. Things are forgotten wholesale. What are the names 'Costanoan', 'Wappo'? They are what the Spanish called

---

* Milan Kundera, *The Book of Laughter and Forgetting*, transl. Michael Henry Heim (New York: Penguin Books, 1981), p. 22.
† Ibid., pp. 234–5.

the people around the Bay Area and in the Napa Valley, but what those people called themselves we do not know: the names were forgotten even before the people were wiped out. There was no past. Tabula rasa.

One of our finest methods of organised forgetting is called discovery. Julius Caesar exemplifies the technique with characteristic elegance in his *Gallic Wars*. 'It was not certain that Britain existed', he says, 'until I went there.'

To whom was it not certain? But what the heathen know doesn't count. Only if godlike Caesar sees it can Britannia rule the waves.

Only if a European discovered or invented it could America exist. At least Columbus had the wit, in his madness, to mistake Venezuela for the outskirts of Paradise. But he remarked on the availability of cheap slave labour in Paradise.

The first chapter of *California: An Interpretive History*, by Professor Walton Bean, contains this paragraph:

The survival of a Stone Age culture in California was not the result of any hereditary biological limitations on the potential of the Indians as a 'race.' They had been geographically and culturally isolated. The vast expanses of oceans, mountains, and deserts had sheltered California from foreign stimulation as well as from foreign conquest . . .

(being isolated from contact and protected from conquest are, you will have noticed, characteristics of utopia),

. . . and even within California the Indian groups were so settled that they had little contact with each other. On the positive side, there was something to be said for their culture just as it was . . . The California Indians had made a successful adaptation to their environment and they had learned to live without destroying each other.*

Professor Bean's excellent book is superior to many of its kind in the area of my particular interest: the first chapter. Chapter 1 of the American history – South or North America, national or regional – is usually short. Unusually short. In it, the 'tribes' that 'occupied' the area are mentioned and perhaps anecdotally described. In Chapter 2, a European 'discovers' the area; and with a gasp of relief the historian plunges into a narration of the conquest, often referred to as settlement or colonisation, and the acts of the conquerors. Since history has traditionally been defined by historians as the written record, this imbalance is inevitable. And in a larger sense it is legitimate; for the non-urban people of the Americas had no history, properly speaking, and therefore are visible only to the anthropologist, not to the historian, except as they entered into white history.

The imbalance is unavoidable, legitimate, and also, I believe, very dangerous. It expresses too conveniently the conquerors' wish to deny the value of the cultures they destroyed, and dehumanize the people they killed. It partakes too much of the method of organised forgetting. To call this 'the New World' – there's a Caesarian birth!

* Walton Bean, *California: An Interpretive History* (New York: McGraw-Hill, 1968), p. 4.

The words 'holocaust' and 'genocide' are fashionable now; but not often are they applied to American history. We were not told in school in Berkeley that the history of California had the final solution for its first chapter. We were told that the Indians 'gave way' before the 'march of progress'.

In the Introduction to *The Wishing Bone Cycle*, Howard A. Norman says:

> The Swampy Cree have a conceptual term which I've heard used to describe the thinking of a porcupine as he backs into a rock crevice:
>
> *Usà puyew usu wapiw!*
>
> 'He goes backward, looks forward.' The porcupine consciously goes backward in order to speculate safely on the future, allowing him to look out at his enemy or the new day. To the Cree, it's an instructive act of self-preservation.[*]

The opening formula for a Cree story is 'an invitation to listen, followed by the phrase "I go backward, look forward, as the porcupine does." '[†]

In order to speculate safely on an inhabitable future, perhaps we would do well to find a rock crevice and go backward. In order to find our roots, perhaps we should look for them where roots are usually found. At least the Spirit of Place is a more benign one than the exclusive and

---

[*] Howard A. Norman, Introduction, *The Wishing Bone Cycle* (New York: Stonehill, 1979).
[†] Ibid.

aggressive Spirit of Race, the mysticism of blood that has cost so much blood. With all our self-consciousness, we have very little sense of where we live, where we are right here right now. If we did, we wouldn't muck it up the way we do. If we did, our literature would celebrate it. If we did, our religion might be participatory. If we did – if we really lived here, now, in this present – we might have some sense of our future as a people. We might know where the centre of the world is.

> . . . Ideally, at its loftiest and most pure, the utopia aspires to (if it has never reached) the condition of the idyll as Schiller describes it – that mode of poetry which would lead man, not back to Arcadia, but forward to Elysium, to a state of society in which man would be at peace with himself and the external world.[*]

The California Indians had made a successful adaptation to their environment, and they had learned to live without destroying each other.[†]

It was Arcadia, of course; it was not Elysium. I heed Victor Turner's warning not to confuse archaic or primitive societies with the true *communitas*, 'which is a dimension of all societies, past and present'.[‡] I am not proposing a return to the Stone Age. My intent is not reactionary, nor even conservative, but simply subversive. It seems that the

[*] Elliott, *Shape of Utopia*, p. 107.
[†] Bean, *California*, p. 4.
[‡] Victor W. Turner, *The Ritual Process: Structure and Anti-Structure* (Chicago: Aldine, 1969), p. 129.

utopian imagination is trapped, like capitalism and industrialism and the human population, in a one-way future consisting only of growth. All I'm trying to do is figure out how to put a pig on the tracks.

Go backward. Turn and return.

If the word [utopia] is to be redeemed, it will have to be by someone who has followed utopia into the abyss which yawns behind the Grand Inquisitor's vision.[*]

The utopia of the Grand Inquisitor

is the product of 'the euclidean mind' (a phrase Dostoyevsky often used), which is obsessed by the idea of regulating all life by reason and bringing happiness to man whatever the cost.[†]

The single vision of the Grand Inquisitor perceives the condition of man in a way stated with awful clarity by Yevgeny Zamyatin, in *We*:

There were two in paradise, and the choice was offered to them: happiness without freedom, or freedom without happiness. No other choice.[‡]

No other choice. Hear now the voice of Urizen!

[*] Elliott, *Shape of Utopia*, p. 100.
[†] Ibid.
[‡] Quoted in ibid., p. 94.

Hidden, set apart in my stern counsels
Reserved for days of futurity,
I have sought for a joy without pain
For a solid without fluctuation

. . .

Lo, I unfold my darkness and on
This rock place with strong hand the book
Of eternal brass, written in my solitude.
Laws of peace, of love, of unity,
Of pity, compassion, forgiveness.
Let each choose one habitation,
His ancient infinite mansion,
One command, one joy, one desire,
One curse, one weight, one measure,
One King, One God, one Law.[*]

In order to believe in utopia, Bob Elliott said, we must believe

that through the exercise of their reason men can control
and in major ways alter for the better their social environment . . . One must have faith of a kind that our history has
made nearly inaccessible.[†]

'When the Way is lost', Lao Tzu observed in a rather similar
historical situation a few thousand years earlier,

there is benevolence. When benevolence is lost, there is
justice. When justice is lost there are the rites. The rites

---

[*] William Blake, *The Book of Urizen*, lines 52–5, 75–84.
[†] Elliott, *Shape of Utopia*, p. 87.

are the end of loyalty and good faith, the beginning of disorder.*

'Prisons', said William Blake, 'are built with stones of Law.'† And coming back to the Grand Inquisitor, we have Milan Kundera restating the dilemma of Happiness versus Freedom:

> Totalitarianism is not only hell, but also the dream of paradise – the age-old dream of a world where everybody would live in harmony, united by a single common will and faith, without secrets from one another . . . If totalitarianism did not exploit these archetypes, which are deep inside us all and rooted deep in all religions, it could never attract so many people, especially during the early phases of its existence. Once the dream of paradise starts to turn into reality, however, here and there people begin to crop up who stand in its way, and so the rulers of paradise must build a little gulag on the side of Eden. In the course of time this gulag grows ever bigger and more perfect, while the adjoining paradise gets ever smaller and poorer.‡

The purer, the more euclidean the reason that builds a utopia, the greater is its self-destructive capacity. I submit that our lack of faith in the benevolence of reason as the controlling power is well founded. We must test and trust our reason, but to have *faith* in it is to elevate it to godhead.

---

* Lao Tzu, *Tao Teh Ching*, Book II, Chapter 38.
† William Blake, *The Marriage of Heaven and Hell*, Book III: 'Proverbs of Heaven and Hell', line 21.
‡ Kundera, *Book of Laughter and Forgetting*, p. 233.

Zeus the Creator takes over. Unruly Titans are sent to the salt mines, and inconvenient Prometheus to the reservation. Earth itself comes to be the wart on the walls of Eden. The rationalist utopia is a power trip. It is a monotheocracy, declared by executive decree, and maintained by willpower; as its premise is progress, not process, it has no habitable present, and speaks only in the future tense. And in the end reason itself must reject it.

> O that I had never drank the wine nor eat the bread
> Of dark mortality, nor cast my view into futurity, nor turned
> My back darkening the present, clouding with a cloud,
> And building arches high and cities, turrets and towers and domes
> Whose smoke destroyed the pleasant garden, and whose running kennels
> Choked the bright rivers . . .
> Then go, O dark futurity! I will cast thee forth from these
> Heavens of my brain, nor will I look upon futurity more.
> I cast futurity away, and turn my back upon that void
> Which I have made, for lo! futurity is in this moment
> . . .
> So Urizen spoke
> . . .
> Then, glorious bright, exulting in his joy,
> He sounding rose into the heavens, in naked majesty,
> In radiant youth . . .*

---

* William Blake, *Vala, or the Four Zoas*, Book IX, lines 162–7, 178–81, 186, 189–91.

That is certainly the high point of this paper. I wish we could follow Urizen in his splendid vertical jailbreak, but it is a route reserved to the major poets and composers. The rest of us must stay down here on the ground, walking in circles, proposing devious side trips, and asking impertinent questions. My question now is: Where is the place Coyote made?

In a paper about teaching utopia, Professor Kenneth Roemer says:

> The importance of this question was forced upon me several years ago in a freshman comp course at the University of Texas at Arlington. I asked the class to write a paper in response to a hypothetical situation: if you had unlimited financial resources and total local, state, and national support, how would you transform Arlington, Texas into utopia? A few minutes after the class had begun to write, one of the students – a mature and intelligent woman in her late thirties – approached my desk. She seemed embarrassed, even upset. She asked, 'What if I believe that Arlington, Texas, *is* utopia?'*

What do you do with *her* in Walden Two?

Utopia has been euclidean, it has been European, and it has been masculine. I am trying to suggest, in an evasive, distrustful, untrustworthy fashion, and as obscurely as I can, that our final loss of faith in that radiant sandcastle may enable our eyes to adjust to a dimmer light and in it perceive another kind of utopia. As this utopia would not be

* Kenneth Roemer, 'Using Utopia to Teach the Eighties', *World Future Society Bulletin*, July–August 1980.

euclidean, European, or masculinist, my terms and images in speaking of it must be tentative and seem peculiar. Victor Turner's antitheses of structure and *communitas* are useful to my attempt to think about it: structure in society, in his terms, is cognitive, *communitas* existential; structure provides a model, *communitas* a potential; structure classifies, *communitas* reclassifies; structure is expressed in legal and political institutions, *communitas* in art and religion.

Communitas breaks in through the interstices of structure, in liminality; at the edges of structure, in marginality; and from beneath structure, in inferiority. It is almost everywhere held to be sacred or 'holy', possibly because it transgresses or dissolves the norms that govern structured or institutionalized relationships and is accompanied by experiences of unprecedented potency.[*]

Utopian thought has often sought to institutionalize or legislate the experience of *communitas*, and each time it has done so it has run up against the Grand Inquisitor.

The activities of a machine are determined by its structure, but the relation is reversed in organisms – organic structure is determined by its processes.[†]

That is Fritjof Capra, providing another useful analogy. If the attempt to provide a structure that will ensure *communitas* is impaled on the horns of its own dilemma, might one not abandon the machine model and have a go at the organic – permitting process to determine structure? But to do so is to go even further than the Anarchists, and to risk not only

[*] Turner, *Ritual Process*, p. 128.

[†] Fritjof Capra, *The Turning Point* (New York: Simon & Schuster, 1982), excerpted in *Science Digest*, April 1982, p. 30.

being called but being in fact regressive, politically naive, Luddite, and anti-rational. Those are real dangers (though I admit that the risk of being accused of not being in the Main Current of Western Thought is one I welcome the opportunity to run). What kind of utopia can come out of these margins, negations, and obscurities?* Who will even recognize it as a utopia? It won't look the way it ought to. It may look very like some kind of place Coyote made after having a conversation with his own dung.

> The symbol which Trickster embodies is not a static one.

Paul Radin speaking. You will recall that the quality of static perfection is an essential element of the non-inhabitability of the euclidean utopia (a point that Bob Elliott discusses with much cogency):

> The symbol which Trickster embodies is not a static one. It contains within itself the promise of differentiation, the

---

* When I was struggling with the writing of this piece, I had not read the four volumes of Robert Nichols's *Daily Lives in Nghsi-Altai* (New York: New Directions, 1977–79). I am glad that I had not, because my thoughts could not then have so freely and fecklessly coincided, collided, and intersected with his. My paper would have been written in the consciousness of the existence of Nghsi-Altai, as Pierre Menard's *Quixote* was written in the consciousness of the existence of Cervantes' *Quixote* and might have been even more different from what it is than Menard's *Quixote* from Cervantes's. But it can be and I hope will be *read* in the consciousness of the existence of Nghsi-Altai; and the fact that Nghsi-Altai is in some respects the very place I was laboriously trying to get to, and yet lies in quite the opposite direction, can only enlarge the use and meaning of my work. Indeed, if this note leads some readers to go find Nghsi-Altai for themselves, the whole thing will have been worthwhile.

promise of god and man. For this reason every generation occupies itself with interpreting Trickster anew. No generation understands him fully but no generation can do without him . . . for he represents not only the undifferentiated and distant past, but likewise the undifferentiated present within every individual . . . If we laugh at him, he grins at us. What happens to him happens to us.[*]

And he never was in Eden, because coyotes live in the New World. Driven forth by the angel with the flaming sword, Eve and Adam lifted their sad heads and saw Coyote, grinning.

Non-European, non-euclidean, non-masculinist: they are all negative definitions, which is all right, but tiresome; and the last is unsatisfactory, as it might be taken to mean that the utopia I'm trying to approach could only be imagined by women – which is possible – or only inhabited by women – which is intolerable. Perhaps the word I need is yin.

Utopia has been yang. In one way or another, from Plato on, utopia has been the big yang motorcycle trip. Bright, dry, clear, strong, firm, active, aggressive, lineal, progressive, creative, expanding, advancing, and hot.

Our civilization is now so intensely yang that any imagination of bettering its injustices or eluding its self-destructiveness must involve a reversal.

> The ten thousand things arise together
> and I watch their return.

[*] Paul Radin, *The Trickster* (New York: Philosophical Library, 1956), p. 168.

They return each to its root.
Returning to one's roots is known as stillness.
Returning to one's destiny is known as the constant.
Knowledge of the constant is known as discernment.
To ignore the constant
is to go wrong, and end in disorder.[*]

To attain the constant, we must return, go round, go inward, go yinward. What would a yin utopia be? It would be dark, wet, obscure, weak, yielding, passive, participatory, circular, cyclical, peaceful, nurturant, retreating, contracting, and cold.

Now on the subject of heat and cold: a reference in *The Shape of Utopia* sent me to a 1960 lecture by Claude Lévi-Strauss, 'The Scope of Anthropology', which so influenced my efforts to think out this paper that I wish to quote from it at some length, with apologies to those of you to whom the passage[†] is familiar. He is speaking of 'primitive' societies.

Although they exist in history, these societies seem to have worked out or retained a certain wisdom which makes them desperately resist any structural modification which might afford history a point of entry into their lives. The societies which have best protected their distinctive character appear to be those concerned above all with persevering in their existence.

[*] Lao Tzu, *Tao Teh Ching*, Book I, Chapter 16.
[†] Claude Lévi-Strauss, *The Scope of Anthropology* (London: Jonathan Cape, 1968), pp. 46–7. Also included in Claude Lévi-Strauss, *Structural Anthropology II* (New York: Basic Books, 1976), pp. 28–30. The version here is my own amalgam of the two translations.

Persevering in one's existence is the particular quality of the organism; it is not a progress towards achievement, followed by stasis, which is the machine's mode, but an interactive, rhythmic, and unstable process, which constitutes an end in itself.

The way in which they exploit the environment guarantees them a modest standard of living as well as the conservation of natural resources. Though various, their rules of marriage reveal to the demographer's eye a common function; to set the fertility rate very low, and to keep it constant. Finally, a political life based upon consent, and admitting of no decisions but those arrived at unanimously, would seem designed to preclude the possibility of calling on that driving force of collective life which takes advantage of the contrast between power and opposition, majority and minority, exploiter and exploited.

Lévi-Strauss is about to make his distinction between the 'hot' societies, which have appeared since the Neolithic Revolution, and in which 'differentiations between castes and between classes are urged without cease, in order that social change and energy may be extracted from them', and the 'cold' societies, self-limited, whose historical temperature is pretty near zero.

The relevance of this beautiful piece of anthropological thinking to my subject is immediately proven by Lévi-Strauss himself, who in the next paragraph thanks Heaven that anthropologists are not expected to predict man's future, but says that if they were, instead of merely extrapolating from our own 'hot' society, they might propose a progressive integration of the best of the 'hot' with the best of the 'cold'.

If I understand him, this unification would involve carrying the Industrial Revolution, already the principal source of social energy, to its logical extreme: the completed Electronic Revolution. After this, change and progress would be strictly cultural and, as it were, machine-made.

> With culture having integrally taken over the burden of manufacturing progress, society . . . placed outside and above history, could once more assume that regular and as it were crystalline structure, which the surviving primitive societies teach us is not antagonistic to the human condition.

The last phrase, from that austere and sombre mind, is poignant.

As I understand it, Lévi-Strauss suggests that to combine the hot and the cold is to transfer mechanical operational modes to machines while retaining organic modes for humanity. Mechanical process; biological rhythm. A kind of superspeed electronic yang train, in whose yin pullmans and dining cars life is serene and the rose on the table does not even tremble. What worries me in this model is the dependence upon cybernetics as the integrating function. Who's up in the engineer's seat? Is it on auto? Who wrote the program – old Nobodaddy Reason again? Is it another of those trains with no brakes?

It may simply be the bad habits of my mind that see in this brief utopian glimpse a brilliant update of an old science-fiction theme: the world where robots do the work while the human beings sit back and play. These were always satirical works. The rule was that either an impulsive young man wrecked the machinery and saved humanity from stagnation, or else the machines, behaving with impeccable logic, did away with the squashy and superfluous people. The first and finest of the lot, E. M. Forster's 'The Machine Stops', ends on a characteristic double chord of terror and promise: the machinery collapses, the crystalline society is shattered with it, but outside there are free people – how civilised, we don't know, but outside and free.

We're back to Kundera's wart on the walls of Eden – the exiles from paradise in whom the hope of paradise lies, the inhabitants of the gulag who are the only free souls. The information systems of the train are marvellous, but the tracks run through Coyote country.

In ancient times the Yellow Emperor first used benevolence and righteousness and meddled with the minds of men. Yao and Shun followed him and worked till there was no more hair on their shins . . . in the practice of benevolence and righteousness, taxed their blood and breath in the establishment of laws and standards. But still some would not submit to their rule, and had to be exiled, driven away . . . The world coveted knowledge . . . there were axes and saws to shape things, ink and plumblines to trim them, mallets and gouges to poke holes in them, and the world, muddled and deranged, was in great confusion.*

That is Chuang Tzu, the first great Trickster of philosophy, sending a raspberry to the Yellow Emperor, the legendary

* *The Complete Works of Chuang Tzu*, transl. Burton Watson (New York: Columbia University Press, 1968), p. 116.

model of rational control. Things were hot in Chuang Tzu's day, too, and he proposed a radical cooling off. The best understanding, he said, 'rests in what it cannot understand. If you do not understand this, then Heaven the Equalizer will destroy you.'*

Having copied out this sentence, I obeyed, letting my understanding rest in what it could not understand, and went to the *I Ching*. I asked that book please to describe a yin utopia for me. It replied with Hexagram 30, the doubled trigram Fire, with a single changing line in the first place taking me to Hexagram 56, the Wanderer. The writing of the rest of this paper and the revisions of it were considerably influenced by a continuing rumination of those texts.

If utopia is a place that does not exist, then surely (as Lao Tzu would say) the way to get there is by the way that is not a way. And in the same vein, the nature of the utopia I am trying to describe is such that if it is to come, it must exist already.

I believe that it does:† most clearly as an element in such deeply unsatisfactory utopian works as Hudson's *A Crystal World* or Aldous Huxley's *Island*. Indeed Bob Elliott ended his book on utopia with a discussion of *Island*. Huxley's 'extraordinary achievement', he says, 'is to have made the old utopian goal – the central human goal – thinkable once

---

* Ibid., p. 254. 'Heaven the Equalizer' was translated by James Legge as 'the Lathe of Heaven', a fine phrase, from which I have got considerable mileage; but Joseph Needham has gently pointed out to me that when Chuang Tzu was writing the Chinese had not yet invented the lathe. Fortunately we now have Burton Watson's wonderfully satisfying translation to turn to.
† In Nghsi-Altai – partly.

more'.* Those are the last words of the book. It is very like Bob that they should not be the closing but the opening of a door.

The major utopic element in my novel *The Dispossessed* is a variety of pacifist anarchism, which is about as yin as a political ideology can get. Anarchism rejects the identification of civilization with the state, and the identification of power with coercion; against the inherent violence of the 'hot' society it asserts the value of such antisocial behaviour as the general refusal of women to bear arms in war, and other coyote devices. In these areas anarchism and Taoism converge both in matter and manner, and so I came there to play my fictional games. The structure of the book may suggest the balance-in-motion and rhythmic recurrence of the Tai Chi, but its excess yang shows: though the utopia was (both in fact and in fiction) founded by a woman, the protagonist is a man; and he dominates it in, I must say, a very masculine fashion. Fond as I am of him, I'm not going to let him talk here. I want to hear a different voice. This is Lord Dorn, addressing the Council of his country, on 16 June 1906. He is talking not to, but about, us.

> With them the son and the father are of different civilizations and are strangers to each other. They move too fast to see more than the surface glitter of a life too swift to be real. They are assailed by too many new things ever to find the depths in the old before it has gone by. The rush of life past them they call progress, though it is too rapid for them to move with it. Man remains the same, baffled and astonished, with a heap of new things around him but gone before he

---

* Elliott, *Shape of Utopia*, p. 153.

knows them. Men may live many sorts of lives, and this they call 'opportunity', and believe opportunity good without ever examining any one of those lives to know if it is good. We have fewer ways of life and most of us never know but one. It is a rich way, and its richness we have not yet exhausted . . . They cannot be blamed for seeing nothing good in us that will be destroyed by them. The good we have they do not understand, or even see.*

Now, this speech might have been made in the council of any non-Western nation or people at the time of its encounter with Europeans in numbers. This could be a Kikuyu talking, or a Japanese — and certainly Japan's decision to Westernize was in the author's mind — and it is almost painfully close to the observations of Black Elk, Standing Bear, Plenty-Coups, and other native North American spokesmen.

Islandia is not a hot but a warm society: it has a definite though flexible class hierarchy, and has adopted some elements of industrial technology; it certainly has been and is conscious of its history, though it has not yet entered into world history, mainly because, like California, it is geographically marginal and remote. In this central debate at the Council of Islandia, the hinge of the book's plot and structure, a deliberate choice is made to get no hotter: to reject the concept of progress as a wrong direction, and to accept persevering in one's existence as a completely worthy social goal.

In how many other utopias is this choice rationally propounded, argued, and made?

---

* Austin Tappan Wright, *Islandia* (New York: Alfred A. Knopf, 1942), p. 490.

It is easy to dismiss *Islandia* as a mere fantasy of the Golden Age, naively escapist or regressive. I believe it is a mistake to do so, and that the options it offers are perhaps more realistic and more urgent than those of most utopias.

Here is Lévi-Strauss once more, this time on the subject of viruses:

> The reality of a virus is almost of an intellectual order. In effect, its organism is reduced practically to the genetic formula that it injects into simple or complex beings, thus forcing their cells to betray their characteristic formula in order to obey its own and to manufacture beings like itself.
>
> In order for our civilization to appear, the previous and simultaneous existence of other civilizations was necessary. And we know, since Descartes, that its originality consists essentially of a method which, because of its intellectual nature, is not suited to generating other civilizations of flesh and blood, but one which can impose its formula on them and force them to become like it. In comparison with these civilizations – whose living art expresses their corporeal quality because it relates to very intense beliefs and, in its conception as much as in its execution, to a certain state of equilibrium between man and nature – does our own civilization correspond to an animal or a viral type?*

This is the virus that Lord Dorn saw carried by the most innocent tourist from Europe or the United States: a plague against which his people had no immunity. Was he wrong?

---

* Lévi-Strauss, 'Art in 1985', in *Structural Anthropology II*, p. 283.

Any small society that tried to make Lord Dorn's choice has, in fact, been forcibly infected; and the big, numerous civilizations – Japan, India, and now China – have either chosen to infect themselves with the viral fever or have failed to make any choice, all too often mixing the most exploitive features of the hot world with the most passive of the cold in a way that almost guarantees the impossibility of their persevering in their own existence of allowing local nature to continue in health. I wanted to speak of *Islandia* because I know no other utopian work that takes for its central intellectual concern this matter of 'Westernization' or 'progress', which is perhaps the central fact of our times. Of course the book provides no answer or solution; it simply indicates the way that cannot be gone. It is an enantiodroma, a *reculer pour mieux sauter*, a porcupine backing into a crevice. It goes sideways. That's very likely why it gets left out of the survey courses in Utopian Lit. But side trips and reversals are precisely what minds stuck in forward gear most need, and in its very quality of forswearing 'futurity', of standing aside – and of having been left aside – *Islandia* is, I suggest, a valuable as well as an endearing book.

It is to some degree a Luddite book as well; and I am forced to now ask: Is it our high technology that gives our civilization its invasive, self-replicating, mechanical forward drive? In itself, technology is 'infectious' only as other useful or impressive elements of culture are; ideas, institutions, fashions too, may be self-replicating and irresistibly imitable. Obviously, technology is an essential element of all cultures and very often, in the form of potsherds or bits of styrofoam, all they leave behind in time. It is far too basic to all civilizations to be characterized in itself as either yin or yang, I think. But at this time, here and now, the continuously progressing character of our technology, and the continuous change that depends upon it – 'the manufacture of progress', as Lévi-Strauss called it – is the principal vehicle of the yang, or 'hotness', of our society.

One need not smash one's typewriter and go bomb the laundromat, after all, because one has lost faith in the continuous advance of technology as the way towards utopia. Technology remains, in itself, an endless creative source. I only wish that I could follow Lévi-Strauss in seeing it as leading from the civilization that turns men into machines to 'the civilization that will turn machines into men'.* But I cannot. I do not see how even the most ethereal technologies promised by electronics and information theory can offer more than the promise of the simplest tool: to make life materially easier, to enrich us. That is a great promise and gain! But if this enrichment of one type of civilization occurs only at the cost of the destruction of the planet, then it seems fairly clear to me that to count upon technological advance for *anything but* technological advance is a mistake. I have not been convincingly shown, and seem to be totally incapable of imagining for myself, how any further technological advance of any kind will bring us any closer to being a society predominantly concerned with preserving its existence; a society with a modest standard of living, conservative of natural resources, with a low constant fertility rate and a political life based upon consent; a society that has made a successful

* Lévi-Strauss, *Scope of Anthropology*, p. 49.

adaptation to its environment and has learned to live without destroying itself or the people next door. But that is the society I want to be able to imagine – I must be able to imagine, for one does not get on without hope.

What are we offered by way of hope? Models, plans, blueprints, wiring diagrams. Prospects of ever more inclusive communications systems linking virus to virus all over the globe – no secrets, as Kundera says. Little closed orbiting test-tubes full of viruses, put up by the L5 Society, in perfect obedience to our compulsion to, as they say, 'build the future' – to be Zeus, to have power over what happens, to control. Knowledge is power, and we want to know what comes next, we want it all mapped out.

Coyote country has not been mapped. The way that cannot be gone is not in the road atlas, or is every road in the atlas.

In the *Handbook of the Indians of California*, A. L. Kroeber wrote, 'The California Indians . . . usually refuse pointblank to make even an attempt [to draw a map], alleging utter inability.'*

The euclidean utopia is mapped; it is geometrically organized, with the parts labeled *a, a', b*: a diagram or model, which social engineers can follow and reproduce. Reproduction, the viral watchword.

In the *Handbook*, discussing the so-called Kuksu Cult or Kuksu Society – a clustering of rites and observances found among the Yuki, Pomo, Maidu, Wintu, Miwok, Costanoan,

---

* Alfred L. Kroeber, *Handbook of the Indians of California*, Smithsonian Institution, *Bureau of American Ethnology Bulletin* 78 (Washington, DC, 1925), p. 344.

and Esselen peoples of Central California – Kroeber observed that our use of the terms 'the cult' or 'a society', our perception of a general or abstract entity, Kuksu, falsifies the native perception:

> The only societies were those of the town unit. They were not branches, because there was no parent stem. Our method, in any such situation, religious or otherwise, is to constitute a central and superior body. Since the day of the Roman empire and the Christian church, we hardly think of a social activity except as it is coherently organized into a definite unit definitely subdivided.
>
> But it must be recognized that such a tendency is not an inherent and inescapable one of all civilization. If we are able to think socially only in terms of an organized machine, the California native was just as unable to think in those terms.
>
> When we recall with how slender a machinery and how rudimentary an organization the whole business of Greek civilization was carried out, it becomes easily intelligible that the . . . Californian could dispense with almost all endeavors in this direction, which to us seem vital.*

Copernicus told us that the earth was not the centre. Darwin told us that man is not the centre. If we listened to the anthropologists we might hear them telling us, with appropriate indirectness, that the white West is not the centre. The centre of the world is a bluff on the Klamath River, a rock in Mecca, a hole in the ground in Greece, nowhere, its circumference everywhere.

* Ibid., p. 374.

Perhaps the utopist should heed this unsettling news at last. Perhaps the utopist would do well to lose the plan, throw away the map, get off the motorcycle, put on a very strange-looking hat, bark sharply three times, and trot off looking thin, yellow, and dingy across the desert and up into the digger pines.

I don't think we're ever going to get to utopia again by going forward, but only roundabout or sideways; because we're in a rational dilemma, an either/or situation as perceived by the binary computer mentality, and neither the either nor the or is a place where people can live. Increasingly often in these increasingly hard times I am asked by people I respect and admire, 'Are you going to write books about the terrible injustice and misery of our world, or are you going to write escapist and consolatory fantasies?' I am urged by some to do one – by some to do the other. I am offered the Grand Inquisitor's choice. Will you choose freedom without happiness, or happiness without freedom? The only answer one can make, I think, is: No.

Back round once more. *Usà puyew usu wapiw!*

If the word [utopia] is to be redeemed, it will have to be by someone who has followed utopia into the abyss which yawns behind the Grand Inquisitor's vision, and who then has clambered out on the other side.*

Sounds like Coyote to me. Falls into things, traps, abysses, and then clambers out somehow, grinning stupidly. Is it possible that we are in fact no longer confronting the Grand

---

* Elliott, *Shape of Utopia*, p. 100.

Inquisitor? Could he be the Father Figure whom we have set up before us? Could it be that by turning around we can put him behind us, and leave him staring like Ozymandias King of Kings out across the death camps, the gulags, the Waste Land, the uninhabitable kingdom of Zeus, the binary-option, single-vision country where one must choose between happiness and freedom?

If so, then we are in the abyss behind him. Not out. A typical Coyote predicament. We have got ourselves into a really bad mess and have got to get out; and we have to be sure that it's the other side we get out to; and when we do get out, we shall be changed.

I have no idea who we will be or what it may be like on the other side, though I believe there are people there. They have always lived there. There are songs they sing there; one of the songs is called 'Dancing at the Edge of the World'. If we, clambering up out of the abyss, ask questions of them, they won't draw maps, alleging utter inability; but they may point. One of them might point in the direction of Arlington, Texas. I live there, she says. See how beautiful it is!

This is the New World! we will cry, bewildered but delighted. We have discovered the New World!

Oh no, Coyote will say. No, this is the old world. The one I made.

You made it for us! we will cry, amazed and grateful.

I wouldn't go so far as to say that, says Coyote.

2

Utopiyin, Utopiyang

These are some thoughts about utopia and dystopia.

The old, crude Good Places were compensatory visions of controlling what you couldn't control and having what you didn't have here and now – an orderly, peaceful heaven; a paradise of houris; pie in the sky. The way to them was clear, but drastic. You died.

Thomas More's secular and intellectual construct *Utopia* was still an expression of desire for something lacking here and now – rational human control of human life – but his Good Place was explicitly No Place. Only in the head. A blueprint without a building site.

Ever since, utopia has been located not in the afterlife but just off the map, across the ocean, over the mountains, in the future, on another planet, a liveable yet unattainable elsewhere.

Every utopia since *Utopia* has also been, clearly or obscurely, actually or possibly, in the author's or in the readers' judgment, both a good place and a bad one. Every eutopia contains a dystopia, every dystopia contains a eutopia.

In the Yang-Yin symbol each half contains within it a portion of the other, signifying their complete interdependence and continual intermutability. The figure is static, but each half contains the seed of transformation. The symbol represents not a stasis but a process.

It may be useful to think of utopia in terms of this long-lived Chinese symbol, particularly if one is willing to forgo the usual masculinist assumption that yang is superior to yin, and instead consider the interdependence and intermutability of the two as the essential feature of the symbol.

Yang is male, bright, dry, hard, active, penetrating. Yin is female, dark, wet, easy, receptive, containing. Yang is control, yin acceptance. They are great and equal powers; neither can exist alone, and each is always in process of becoming the other.

Both utopia and dystopia are often an enclave of maximum control surrounded by a wilderness – as in Butler's *Erewhon*, E. M. Forster's 'The Machine Stops' and Yevgeny Zamyatin's *We*. Good citizens of utopia consider the wilderness dangerous, hostile, unliveable; to an adventurous or rebellious dystopian it represents change and freedom. In this I see examples of the intermutability of the yang and yin: the dark, mysterious wilderness surrounding a bright, safe place, the Bad Places – which then become the Good Place, the bright, open future surrounding a dark, closed prison . . . Or vice versa.

In the last half-century this pattern has been repeated perhaps to exhaustion, variations on the theme becoming more and more predictable, or merely arbitrary.

Notable exceptions to the pattern are Huxley's *Brave New World*, a eudystopia in which the wilderness has been reduced to an enclave so completely dominated by the intensely controlled yang world-state that any hope of its offering freedom or change is illusory; and Orwell's *1984*, a pure dystopia in which the yin element has been totally eliminated by the yang, appearing only in the receptive obedience of the controlled masses and as manipulated delusions of wilderness and freedom.

Yang, the dominator, always seeks to deny its dependence on yin. Huxley and Orwell uncompromisingly present the outcome of successful denial. Through psychological and political control, these dystopias have achieved a nondynamic stasis that allows no change. The balance is immovable: one side up, the other down. Everything is yang forever.

Where is the yin dystopia? Is it perhaps in post-holocaust stories and horror fiction with its shambling herds of zombies, the increasingly popular visions of social breakdown, total loss of control – chaos and old night?

Yang perceives yin only as negative, inferior, bad, and yang has always been given the last word. But there is no last word.

At present we seem only to write dystopias. Perhaps in order to be able to write a utopia we need to think yinly. I tried to write one in *Always Coming Home*. Did I succeed?

Is a yin utopia a contradiction in terms, since all the familiar utopias rely on control to make them work, and yin does not control? Yet it is a great power. How does it work?

I can only guess. My guess is that the kind of thinking we are, at last, beginning to do about how to change the goals of human domination and unlimited growth to those of human adaptability and long-term survival is a shift from yang to yin, and so involves acceptance of impermanence and imperfection, a patience with uncertainty and the makeshift, a friendship with water, darkness, and the earth.

3

A War Without End

———⟫·◈·⟪———

Some thoughts, written down at intervals, about oppression, revolution, and imagination.

Slavery

My country came together in one revolution and was nearly broken by another.

The first revolution was a protest against galling, stupid, but relatively mild social and economic exploitation. It was almost uniquely successful.

Many of those who made the first revolution practiced the most extreme form of economic exploitation and social oppression: they were slave owners.

The second American revolution, the Civil War, was an attempt to preserve slavery. It was partially successful. The institution was abolished, but the mind of the master and the mind of the slave still think a good many of the thoughts of America.

Resistance to Oppression

Phillis Wheatley, poet and manumitted slave, wrote in 1774: 'In every human Breast, God has implanted a principle, which we call Love of Freedom; it is impatient of Oppression, and pants for Deliverance.'

I would no more deny the truth of that than I would deny that the sun shines. All that is good in the institutions and politics of my country rests on it.

And yet I see that though we love freedom we are mostly patient of oppression, and even refuse deliverance.

I see a danger in insisting that our love of freedom always outweighs whatever force or inertia keeps us from resisting oppression and seeking deliverance.

If I deny that strong, intelligent, capable people will and do accept oppression, I'm identifying the oppressed as weak, stupid, and inept.

If it were true that superior people refuse to be treated as inferiors, it would follow that those low in the social order are truly inferior, since, if they were superior, they'd protest; since they accept an inferior position, they are inferior. This is the comfortably tautological argument of the slave-owner, the social reactionary, the racist, and the misogynist.

It is an argument that still bedevils consideration of the Hitlerian holocaust: Why did the Jews 'just get into the trains'? Why didn't they 'fight back'? A question which – as asked – is unanswerable, and so can be used by the anti-Semite to imply the inferiority of the Jews.

But the argument appeals also to the idealist. Many liberal and humanely conservative Americans cherish the conviction that all oppressed people suffer intolerably from their oppression, must be ready and eager to rebel, and are morally weak, morally wrong, if they do not rebel.

I categorically judge as wrong any person who considers himself or herself racially or socially superior to another or enforces inferior status on another. But it is a different matter to pass categorical judgment against people who accept inferior status. If I say that they are wrong, that morality demands that they rebel, it behoves me to consider what real choice they have, whether they act in ignorance or through conviction, whether they have any opportunity to lessen their ignorance or change their conviction. Having so considered, how can I say they are at fault? Is it they, and not the oppressors, who do wrong?

The ruling class is always small, the lower orders large, even in a caste society. The poor always vastly outnumber the rich. The powerful are fewer than those they hold power over. Adult men hold superior status in almost all societies, though they are always outnumbered by women and children. Governments and religions sanction and uphold inequality, social rank, gender rank, and privilege, wholly or selectively.

Most people, in most places, in most times, are of inferior status.

And most people, even now, even in 'the free world', even in 'the home of the free', consider this state of affairs, or certain elements of it, as natural, necessary, and unchangeable. They hold it to be the way it has always been and therefore the way it must be. This may be conviction or it may be ignorance; often it is both. Over the centuries, most people of inferior status have had no way of knowing that any other way of ordering society has existed or could exist – that change is possible. Only those of superior status have ever known enough to know that; and it is their power and privilege that would be at stake if the order of things were changed.

We cannot trust history as a moral guide in these matters, because history is written by the superior class, the educated, the empowered. But we have only history to go on, and observation of current events. On that evidence, revolt and rebellion are rare things, revolution extremely rare. In most times, in most places, most women, slaves, serfs, low-castes, outcastes, peasants, working-class people, most people defined as inferior – that is, most people – have not rebelled against being despised and exploited. They resist, yes; but their resistance is likely to be passive, or so devious, so much a part of daily behaviour, as to be all but invisible.

When voices from the oppressed and the underclasses are recorded, some are cries for justice, but most are expressions of patriotism, cheers for the king, vows to defend the father-land, all loyally supporting the system that disenfranchises them and the people who profit from it.

Slavery would not have existed all over the world if slaves often rose against their masters. Most slave-masters are not murdered. They are obeyed.

Working men watch their company's CEOs get paid three hundred times what they are paid, and grumble, but do nothing.

Women in most societies uphold the claims and institutions of male supremacy, deferring to men, obeying them (overtly), and defending the innate superiority of men as natural fact or religious dogma.

Low-status males – young men, poor men – fight and die for the system that keeps them under. Most of the countless soldiers killed in the countless wars waged to uphold the power of a society's rulers or religion have been men considered inferior by that society.

'You have nothing to lose but your chains', but we prefer to kiss them.

Why?

Are human societies inevitably constructed as a pyramid, with the power concentrating at the top? Is a hierarchy of power a biological imperative that human society is bound to enact? The question is almost certainly wrongly phrased and so impossible to answer, but it keeps getting asked and answered, and those who ask it usually answer it in the affirmative.

If such an inborn, biological imperative exists, is it equally imperative in both sexes? We have no incontrovertible evidence of innate gender difference in social behaviour. Essentialists on both sides of the argument maintain that men are innately disposed to establish a power hierarchy while women, though they do not initiate such structures, accept or imitate them. According to the essentialists, the male programme is thus certain to prevail, and we should expect to find the chain of command, the 'higher' commanding the 'lower', with power concentrated in a few, a nearly universal pattern of human society.

Anthropology provides some exceptions to this supposed universality. Ethnologists have described societies that have no fixed chain of command; in them power, instead of being locked into a rigid system of inequality, is fluid, shared differently in different situations, operating by checks and balances tending always towards consensus. They have described societies that do not rank one gender as superior, though there is always some gendered division of labour, and male pursuits are those most likely to be celebrated.

But these are all societies we describe as 'primitive' – tautologically, since we have already established a value hierarchy: primitive = low = weak, civilized = high = powerful.

Many 'primitive' and all 'civilized' societies are rigidly stratified, with much power assigned to a few and little or no power to most. Is the perpetuation of institutions of social inequality in fact the engine that drives civilization, as Lévi-Strauss suggests?

People in power are better fed, better armed, and better educated, and therefore better able to stay that way, but is that sufficient to explain the ubiquity and permanence of extreme social inequality? Certainly the fact that men are slightly larger and more muscular (though somewhat less durable) than women is not sufficient to explain the ubiquity of gender inequality and its perpetuation in societies where size and muscularity do not make much difference.

If human beings hated injustice and inequality as we say we do and think we do, would any of the Great Empires and High Civilizations have lasted fifteen minutes?

If we Americans hate injustice and inequality as passionately as we say we do, would any person in this country lack enough to eat?

We demand a rebellious spirit of those who have no chance to learn that rebellion is possible, but we the privileged hold still and see no evil.

We have good reason to be cautious, to be quiet, not to rock the boat. A lot of peace and comfort is at stake. The mental and moral shift from denial of injustice to consciousness of injustice is often made at very high cost. My contentment, stability, safety, personal affections, may become a sacrifice to the dream of the common good, to the idea of a freedom that I may not live to share, an ideal of justice that nobody may ever attain.

The last words of the *Mahabharata* are, 'By no means can I attain a goal beyond my reach.' It is likely that justice, a human idea, is a goal beyond human reach. We're good at inventing things that can't exist.

Maybe freedom cannot be attained through human institutions but must remain a quality of the mind or spirit not dependent on circumstances, a gift of grace. This (if I understand it) is the religious definition of freedom. My problem with it is that its devaluation of work and circumstance encourages institutional injustices which make the gift of grace inaccessible. A two-year-old child who dies of starvation or a beating or a firebombing has not been granted access to freedom, nor any gift of grace, in any sense in which I can understand the words.

We can attain by our own efforts only an imperfect justice, a limited freedom. Better than none. Let us hold fast to that principle, the love of Freedom, of which the freed slave, the poet, spoke.

The Ground of Hope

The shift from denial of injustice to recognition of injustice can't be unmade.

What your eyes have seen they have seen. Once you see the injustice, you can never again in good faith deny the oppression and defend the oppressor. What was loyalty is now betrayal. From now on, if you don't resist, you collude.

But there is a middle ground between defence and attack, a ground of flexible resistance, a space opened for change. It is not an easy place to find or live in. Peacemakers trying to get there have ended up scuttling in panic to Munich.

Even if they reach the middle ground, they may get no thanks for it. Harriet Beecher Stowe's Uncle Tom is a slave who, for his courageous effort to persuade his owner to change his heart and his steadfast refusal to beat other slaves, is beaten to death. We insist on using him as a symbol of cringing capitulation and servility.

Admiring heroically useless defiance, we sneer at patient resistance.

But the negotiating ground, where patience makes change, is where Gandhi stood. Lincoln got there, painfully. Bishop Tutu, having lived there for years in singular honour, saw his country move, however awkwardly and uncertainly, towards that ground of hope.

The Master's Tools

Audre Lord said you can't dismantle the master's house with the master's tools. I think about this powerful metaphor, trying to understand it.

By radicals, liberals, conservatives, and reactionaries, education in the masters' knowledge is seen as leading *inevitably* to consciousness of oppression and exploitation, and so to the subversive desire for equality and justice.

Liberals support and reactionaries oppose universal free education, public schools, uncensored discussion at the universities for exactly the same reason.

Lord's metaphor seems to say that education is irrelevant to social change. If nothing the master used can be useful to the slave, then education in the masters' knowledge must be abandoned. Thus an underclass must entirely reinvent society, achieve a new knowledge, in order to achieve justice. If they don't, the revolution will fail.

This is plausible. Revolutions generally fail. But I see their failure beginning when the attempt to rebuild the house so everybody can live in it becomes an attempt to grab all the saws and hammers, barricade Ole Massa's tool-room, and keep the others out. Power not only corrupts, it addicts. Work becomes destruction. Nothing is built.

Societies change with and without violence. Reinvention is possible. Building is possible. What tools have we to build with except hammers, nails, saws – education, learning to think, learning skills?

Are there indeed tools that have not been invented, which we must invent in order to build the house we want our children to live in? Can we go on from what we know now, or does what we know now keep us from learning what we need to know? To learn what people of colour, the women, the poor, have to teach, to learn the knowledge we need, must we unlearn all the knowledge of the whites, the men, the powerful? Along with the priesthood and phallocracy, must we throw away science and democracy? Will we be left trying to build without any tools but our bare hands? The metaphor is rich and dangerous. I can't answer the questions it raises.

Only in Utopias

In the sense that it offers a glimpse of some imagined alternative to 'the way we live now', much of my fiction can be called utopian, but I continue to resist the word. Many of my invented societies strike me as an improvement in one way or another on our own, but I find utopia far too grand and too rigid a name for them. Utopia, and dystopia, are intellectual places. I write from passion and playfulness. My stories are neither dire warnings nor blueprints for what we ought to do. Most of them, I think, are comedies of human manners, reminders of the infinite variety of ways in which we always come back to pretty much the same place, and celebrations of that infinite variety by the invention of still more alternatives and possibilities. Even the novels *The Dispossessed* and *Always Coming Home*, in which I worked out more methodically than usual certain variations on the uses of power, which I preferred to those that obtain in our world – even these are as much efforts to subvert as to display the ideal of an attainable social plan which would end injustice and inequality once and for all.

To me the important thing is not to offer any specific hope of betterment but, by offering an imagined but persuasive alternative reality, to dislodge my mind, and so the reader's mind, from the lazy, timorous habit of thinking that the way we live now is the only way people can live. It is that inertia that allows the institutions of injustice to continue unquestioned.

Fantasy and science fiction in their very conception offer alternatives to the reader's present, actual world. Young people in general welcome this kind of story because in their vigour and eagerness for experience they welcome alternatives, possibilities, change. Having come to fear even the imagination of true change, many adults refuse all imaginative literature, priding themselves on seeing nothing beyond what they already know, or think they know.

Yet, as if it feared its own troubling powers, much science fiction and fantasy is timid and reactionary in its social invention, fantasy clinging to feudalism, science fiction to military and imperial hierarchy. Both usually reward their hero, whether a man or woman, only for doing outstandingly manly deeds. (I wrote this way for years myself. In *The Left Hand of Darkness*, my hero is genderless but his heroics are almost exclusively manly.) In science fiction particularly, one also often meets the idea I discussed above, that anyone of inferior status, if not a rebel constantly ready to seize freedom through daring and violent action, is either despicable or simply of no consequence.

In a world so morally simplified, if a slave is not Spartacus, he is nobody. This is merciless and unrealistic. Most slaves, most oppressed people, are part of a social order which, by the very terms of their oppression, they have no opportunity even to perceive as capable of being changed.

The exercise of imagination is dangerous to those who profit from the way things are because it has the power to show that the way things are is not permanent, not universal, not necessary.

Having that real though limited power to put established institutions into question, imaginative literature has also the responsibility of power. The storyteller is the truth-teller.

It is sad that so many stories that might offer a true vision settle for patriotic or religious platitude, technological miracle working, or wishful thinking, the writers not trying to imagine truth. The fashionably noir dystopia merely reverses the platitudes and uses acid instead of saccharine, while still evading engagement with human suffering and with genuine possibility. The imaginative fiction I admire presents alternatives to the status quo which not only question the ubiquity and necessity of extant institutions, but enlarge the field of social possibility and moral understanding. This may be done in as naively hopeful a tone as the first three *Star Trek* television series, or through such complex, sophisticated, and ambiguous constructions of thought and technique as the novels of Philip K. Dick or Carol Emshwiller; but the movement is recognizably the same – the impulse to make change imaginable.

We will not know our own injustice if we cannot imagine justice. We will not be free if we do not imagine freedom. We cannot demand that anyone try to attain justice and freedom who has not had a chance to imagine them as attainable.

I want to close and crown these inconclusive meditations with the words of a writer who never spoke anything but truth, and always spoke it quietly, Primo Levi, who lived a year in Auschwitz, and knew what injustice is.

> The ascent of the privileged, not only in the Lager but in all human coexistence, is an anguishing but unfailing phenomenon: only in utopias is it absent. It is the duty of righteous men to make war on all undeserved privilege, but one must not forget that this is a war without end.

4

The Operating Instructions

<hr/>

I wrote this piece in 2000 as a talk to a group of people interested in local literacy and literature.

A poet has been appointed ambassador. A playwright is elected president. Construction workers stand in line with officer managers to buy a new novel. Adults seek moral guidance and intellectual challenge in stories about warrior monkeys, one-eyed giants, and crazy knights who fight windmills. Literacy is considered a beginning, not an end.

. . . Well, maybe in some other country, but not this one. In America the imagination is generally looked on as something that might be useful when the TV is out of order. Poetry and plays have no relation to practical politics. Novels are for students, housewives, and other people who don't work. Fantasy is for children and primitive peoples. Literacy is so you can read the operating instructions.

I think the imagination is the single most useful tool humankind possesses. It beats the opposable thumb. I can imagine living without my thumbs, but not without my imagination.

I hear voices agreeing with me. 'Yes, yes!' they cry – 'the creative imagination is a tremendous plus in business! We value creativity, we *reward* it!' In the marketplace, the word *creativity* has come to mean the generation of ideas applicable to practical strategies to make larger profits. This reduction has gone on so long that the word *creative* can hardly be degraded further. I don't use it any more, yielding it to capitalists and academics to abuse as they like. But they can't have *imagination*.

Imagination is not a means of making money. It has no place in the vocabulary of profit-making. It is not a weapon, though all weapons originate from it, and the use, or nonuse, of all weapons depends on it: as do all tools and their uses. The imagination is a fundamental way of thinking, an essential means of becoming and remaining human. It is a tool of the mind.

Therefore we have to learn to use it. Children have imagination to start with, as they have body, intellect, the capacity for language: all things essential to their humanity, things they need to learn how to use, how to use well. Such teaching, training, and practice should begin in infancy and go on throughout life. Young human beings need exercise in imagination as they need exercise in all the basic skills of life, bodily and mental: for growth, for health, for competence, for joy. This need continues as long as the mind is alive.

When children are taught to hear and learn the central literature of their people, or, in literate cultures, to read and understand it, their imagination is getting a very large part of the exercise it needs.

Nothing else does as well, not even the other arts. We are a wordy species. Words are the wings both intellect and imagination fly on. Music, dance, visual arts, crafts of all kinds, all are central to human development and well-being, and no art or skill is ever useless learning; but to train the mind to take off from immediate reality and return to it with new understanding and new strength, there is nothing like poem and story.

Through story, every culture defines itself and teaches its children how to be people and members of their people – Hmong, !Kung, Hopi, Quechua, French, Californian . . . We are those who arrived at the Fourth World . . . We are Joan's nation . . . We are the sons of the Sun . . . We came from the sea . . . We are the people who live at the centre of the world.

A people that doesn't live at the centre of the world, as defined and described by its poets and storytellers, is in a bad way. The centre of the world is where you live. You can breathe the air there. You know how things are done there, how things are done rightly, done well.

A child who doesn't know where the centre is – where home is, *what* home is – that child is in a very bad way.

Home isn't Mom and Dad and Sis and Bud. Home isn't where they have to let you in. It's not a place at all. Home is imaginary.

Home, imagined, comes to be. It is real, realer than any other place, but you can't get to it unless your people show you how to imagine it – whoever your people are. They may not be your relatives. They may never have spoken your language. They may have been dead for a thousand years. They may be nothing but words printed on paper, ghosts of voices, shadows of minds. But they can guide you home. They are your human community.

All of us have to learn how to invent our lives, make them up, imagine them. We need to be taught these skills; we need guides to show us how. If we don't, our lives get made up for us by other people.

Human beings have always joined in groups to imagine how best to live and help one another carry out the plan. The essential function of human community is to arrive at some agreement on what we need, what life ought to be, what we want our children to learn, and then collaborate in learning and teaching so that we and they can go on the way we think is the right way.

Small communities with strong traditions are usually clear about the way they want to go, and good at teaching it. But tradition may crystallize imagination to the point of fossilizing it as dogma and forbidding new ideas. Larger communities, such as cities, open up room for people to imagine alternatives, learn from people of different traditions, and invent their own ways to live.

As alternatives proliferate, however, those who take the responsibility of teaching find little social and moral consensus on what they should be teaching – what we need, what life ought to be. In our time of huge populations exposed continuously to reproduced voices, images, and words used for commercial and political profit, there are too many people who want to and can invent us, own us, shape and control us through seductive and powerful media. It's a lot to ask of a child to find a way through all that, alone.

Nobody can do anything very much, really, alone.

What a child needs, what we all need, is to find some other people who have imagined life along lines that make sense and allow some freedom, and listen to them. Not hear passively, but listen.

Listening is an act of community, which takes space, time, and silence.

Reading is a means of listening.

Reading is not as passive as hearing or viewing. It's an act: you do it. You read at your pace, your own speed, not the ceaseless, incoherent, gabbling, shouting rush of the media. You take in what you can and want to take in, not what they shove at you so fast and hard and loud that you're overwhelmed. Reading a story, you may be told something, but you're not being sold anything. And though you're usually alone when you read, you are in communion with another mind. You aren't being brainwashed or co-opted or used; you've joined in an act of the imagination.

I know no reason why the media could not create a similar community of the imagination, as theatre has often done in societies of the past, but they're not doing it. They are so controlled by advertising and profiteering that the best people who work in them, the real artists, if they resist the pressure to sell out, get drowned out by the endless rush for novelty, by the greed of the entrepreneurs.

Much of literature remains free of such co-optation simply because a lot of books were written by dead people, who by definition are not greedy.

And many living poets and novelists, though their publishers may be crawling abjectly after bestsellers, continue to be motivated less by the desire for gain than by the wish to do what they'd probably do for nothing if they could afford it, that is, practise their art — make something well, get something right. Books remain comparatively, and amazingly, honest and reliable.

They may not be 'books', of course, they may not be ink on wood pulp but a flicker of electronics in the palm of a hand. Incoherent and commercialized and worm-eaten with porn and hype and blather as it is, electronic publication offers those who read a strong new means of active community. The technology is not what matters. Words are what matter. The sharing of words. The activation of imagination through the reading of words.

The reason literacy is important is that literature *is* the operating instructions. The best manual we have. The most useful guide to the country we're visiting, life.